Night Sky Frequencies

New and Selected Poems

Night Sky Frequencies

New and Selected Poems

Debra Nystrom

Sheep Meadow Press
Rhinebeck, NY

Designed and typeset by The Sheep Meadow Press

Distributed by The University Press of New England

Cover image from a box of stuff found in Joseph Cornell's attic
Author photo by Mia O'Neill

Library of Congress Cataloging-in-Publication Data

Names: Nystrom, Debra, author.
Title: Night sky frequencies : new and selected poems / Debra Nystrom.
Description: Rhinebeck, NY : Sheep Meadow Press, [2016]
Identifiers: LCCN 2015039473 | ISBN 9781937679590 (softcover)
Classification: LCC PS3564.Y78 A6 2016 | DDC 811/.54--dc23
LC record available at http://lccn.loc.gov/2015039473

All inquiries and permission requests should be addressed to the publisher:

The Sheep Meadow Press
PO Box 84
Rhinebeck, NY 12514

Acknowledgments

I am grateful to the editors of the following magazines and publications, in which these poems from *Night Sky Frequencies* first appeared, some in earlier versions:

AGNI: "What We Believed"

The Cortland Review: "Memory From the First House"

Ecotone: "Recess and the Speed of Sound"

Harvard Review Online: "Star Quilt, and Starfish Sent From a Distant Place, Balanced Against Window Glass"

The Hollins Critic: "Road North"

The New Yorker: "Pronghorn"

North American Review: "Heaven Map," "Dream of the Box Maker's Dream," "Dream: the Box Maker and His Brother"

One: "Shadow Box"

South Dakota Review: "Sioux Falls: Visitation"

Virginia Quarterly Review: "Our Mother Wanted It All to be Beautiful"

Monticello in Mind: "Green-Winged Teals"

32 Poems: "That'll Be the Day"

My heartfelt gratitude to Stanley Moss and The Sheep Meadow Press for their belief in these poems and their work on *Night Sky Frequencies* and *A Quarter Turn*. Sincere thanks also to Sarah Gorham and Sarabande Books for publishing *Torn Sky* and *Bad River Road*.

Thanks are due as well to the editors of the following publications, in which poems from the earlier collections appeared: *AGNI, The American Poetry Review, Anthropology and Humanism, The Bellingham Review, The Best American Poetry 2007* (Scribners, 2008), *Common Wealth* (University of Virginia Press, 2003), *Crazyhorse, Five Fingers Review, Five Points, Greensboro Review, Heart, Indiana Review, Like Thunder: Poets Respond to Violence in America* (University of Iowa Press, 2002), *Lyric, Northwest Review, Orion, Ploughshares, Poetry Daily, Prairie Schooner, Quarterly West, Raccoon, Seneca Review, The Seattle Review, Shenandoah, Slate, The Southeast Review, The Southwest Review, The Threepenny Review, TriQuarterly, The Virginia Quarterly Review, When She Named Fire* (Autumn House Press, 2008), and *Yale Review*.

I would like to express my appreciation to Yaddo, and to The University of Virginia and The Virginia Foundation for the Humanities, for grants that funded time and research for some of this work.

And for their suggestions and support, my deepest thanks to Dan O'Neill, Michael Collier, Lisa Russ Spaar, Ann Beattie, David Wojahn, Carol Muske-Dukes, Mia O'Neill and Max McDonough.

For Dan and Mia, for the Spiel family,

and in memory of Brad and Ellie

CONTENTS

III   NIGHT SKY FREQUENCIES

from A QUARTER TURN (1991)

from TORN SKY (2003)

from BAD RIVER ROAD (2009)

NIGHT SKY FREQUENCIES

Take him and cut him out in little stars,

And he will make the face of heaven so fine

That all the world will be in love with night

And pay no worship to the garish sun.

—Romeo and Juliet, Act III, Scene II

I thought, everything can be used in a lifetime, can't it, and went on walking.

–Joseph Cornell

I   INLAND SEA

NAMES DISAPPEARING, DAKOTA

Day by day the Missouri dropping lower under empty sky
that had drained Okobojo, No Heart Creek, Whiteman Draw; every
night still no moisture. Finally, a season late, the raw
parched air turned and gathered over hardpan above Oahe,
grumbling then breaking open all at once, sending runnels across the flats
to spread and join and drag toward the river's edge snatches of roots
torn from ground where wind had settled the seeds once. Afterwards
Will and Ellie, tromping in mud, scanned the rutted cow-paths for arrowheads
that might've surfaced—traces of Black Buffalo, Big Foot,
Touch the Clouds—quartz or chert or flint notched, chipped to different
sizes and points for buffalo, deer, pheasant flushed out with a human howl,
maybe with fire lit to the grasses, bitter scent of ash twisting in dust Ellie could smell
like her own name unraveling, as she poked a glittering rock
with her stick, heard the meadowlark's question change to sputter, last flick
of wings. Whatever she and Will might lift, turn over in their hands, take home,
hide among their things—even relief after rain did not belong to them.

ELLIE: DREAM OF MY MOTHER AS A GIRL

But she's saying my name—*Ellie*—looking back over her shoulder, face
and arms freshly blistered from the clorox-
scrubbing that her Sorenson grandma's tried again, to erase
the dark skin. As if knowing already it's not safe here, she walks
away, like she did after Dad's arrest. The two of them couldn't
stay happy, but he knocked a man down who never got up again, who'd insulted her
in a Pierre bar where selling alcohol to Indians had been illegal not
so long before. She promised us kids she'd come get us again, said we were
all she'd come for, and now she's looking back to me: *Ellie, make sure
Willy's all right* her look means. I can't say I don't know where he is, rubber band
holding his few letters together, no word if his shot hand works now, or
how he got discharged without destination from an army hospital the other end
of the world—*I just want Willy to be ok* the girl-Mom who doesn't yet know him
or me is saying, and though I can't speak I promise he will be, in the dream.

LONG VISIT

When Dad didn't come back, Mom took us to our cousins' to stay
till she could find another place. *You'll be okay with Aunt Ruthie*
she said in a voice too high. We watched the car and its dust turn
north, beyond the leafless windbreak, then Willy clicked open
our green suitcase, match to the bigger one in Mom's
trunk—pulled out the jumble of plastic Indians
and Cavalry that Dad had given him at Christmas.
He looked around and whispered to me, so I asked
if he could use the quilt in Annie and Lena's bedroom,
to make a bunched-up battle scene—tan braves and blue
soldiers kneeling on ridges, lying behind bluffs, stalking
down ravines, each figure pointing a bow or gun
whichever way he turned, except one—the maiden in a dress
of molded fringed buckskin, who never got hit. *I don't use her unless
Ellie plays*, he said to Annie and Lena. *There's two of every guy, but
not of her.—You can be her if you want*, he offered, and set her apart.
Then gunshot sounded,
arrows whizzed all around, one by one each man took down
some twin, and then in turn got ambushed, bit the dust.
New quilt-rumples, new battles, chaos, loss, the causes mysterious.

DREAM: FATHER GONE

He was patient, teaching me to cast, making sure I got the hang
of it finally, then going a little ways apart, up the creek with his
own pole, keeping quiet. All I wanted was to watch fish
move through shadows inside the stream, nosing
my lure, then feinting, flashing away, knowing they should leave
its strangeness be, as I let them be, let them play under fringe
of weeds and bug-whine, cloudless daylight carrying reflections
where nobody could see, not even him from his spot above,
far up the bank—then gone when I looked, water risen like thick night
—the outlines of my body too disappearing into it, yet feeling a hand
touch my lips, meaning *hush—you'll find*
your way in the dark, once stars come out.

ROAD NORTH

Just north of the Missouri's switchback, a lone cottonwood, like a sudden

mirage of rain, shimmers silver undersides of leaves all day

in the prairie wind. Only tree for miles: at evening a family

of buzzards darkens it till daylight carries them off again—

graceful in the air, black skimmers revolving

on thermals, tilting, scanning for a fox or coyote to follow—

but down on the ground they're hissing, hopping, hitching side to

side, finishing off shreds of what something else has put an end

to, till the great wings flop and lift, glide without a beat again, surveying.

One after another at dusk they settle themselves

back in with last flaps, quiet their tree above the road that curves

around Hand-Stone Bend, heads due north along

homestead-grids, rising and dropping all the way to Canada between

wheat fields. A few hours of dust in that direction, a fugitive could be gone.

WHAT WE BELIEVED

Down the prickly cow path to the creek
we journeyed as if we were insects
making our way along scars
in the hide of a buffalo whose fur brushed us

when the wind passed like a tide across the high grasses
down the prickly cow path to the creek
in chigger-shade where thoughts of time
making our way along scars

lost what they meant up at the house
when the wind passed like a tide across the high grasses
we pulled from our pockets matches swiped
in chigger-shade where thoughts of time

tasting of sulfur at the tips
lost what they meant up at the house
listening to bug-hum and bird-chatter and watching bubbles
we pulled from our pockets matches swiped

the surface of the water trembling
tasting of sulfur at the tips
once by the creek we found rocks with shells in them
listening to bug-hum and bird-chatter and watching bubbles

then carried the rocks back for Uncle Ralph to examine
the surface of the water trembling
the prairie had been a giant sea he told us
once by the creek we found rocks with shells in them

Grandma June says everything was sky not sea I said
then carried the rocks back for Uncle Ralph to examine
none of us sure what we believed
the prairie had been a giant sea he told us

we journeyed as if we were insects
Grandma June says everything was sky not sea I said
in the hide of a buffalo whose fur brushed us
none of us sure what we believed

COUSINS, WHISPERING

Stories for where Will's and my folks had gone, how long they'd
leave us at our cousins' farm—clues puzzled out and weighed
with Annie and Lena in the back closet, where anything
ruined got hidden or else transformed, like the lace torn down in a long
loose spiral from the dress Grandma never wore—
changed to gossamer lining for the fusty nest where we stored
chokecherries, marshmallows, seven arrowheads in a drawstring
bag, pheasant feathers to tuck around the runty kittens not getting
milk enough from wild, scattered mothers. We bundled their scratchy
paws in rags, let down the raspy tongues to jar-lids of whey
sneaked from the porch, then took turns petting the squirmy bodies till
everything was quiet in the shadows of old clothes. We kept still
in the barn's dimness too, beneath the tool-bench, breathing dust and machine
oil like the collies, and the horses brushing flies with their tails, listening
to the men gamble on weather, take apart some engine to see what was wrong,
then put it together again, cigarettes burning to nothing.

RECESS AND THE SPEED OF SOUND

Middle of nowhere: rattling restlessness trembling the window-glass,

and boys look up from marbles on the playground,

their tobacco-bag booty of round

gems spilled, placed to crack one against another at angles across

circles drawn in dirt. Cats' eyes, oilies, steelies—stored beneath beds

at night, while dreams line up precision shots to hold

breath above: perfect-spun explosions; worlds displaced. They've been told

no coin-flips, no betting. Jets from the base shear daily over their heads,

shuddering ground, riffling the grasses. Timmy's uncle in the Air Force

has climbed down into missile silos that hold the Titans over by Pine

Ridge—*the Big Boys are out there under pastures and wind, waiting*

for their chance. Stopping banter now to notice

crows flapping off all at once, kids knuckle down and wait for a bone-

thudding boom to shake their game, make what's precious change hands.

OUR MOTHER WANTED IT ALL TO BE BEAUTIFUL

where we first lived, though the land was for bunchgrass, for

cattle grazing against the wind—not color,

not contented gazing. She dragged the hose, cleared and coaxed hour

after hour in the patch north of the house that Dad let her

do with what she wanted to—fight

the parched air with columbine and rows

of gladiolas, violet-veined irises, moss-roses like a secret

blown in from some sea she'd never see. By the back door, yellow-

and-blood-red snapdragons leaned out from the siding: she showed me

how to pinch them so they'd open like fierce little mouths.

Sunflowers craned up under the east awning; peonies

along the shadeless south burst overnight—fireworks flung out

from tight-fisted, ant-crawling buds. I didn't know then all the names

of flowers, or directions around the yard she dug and tended;

I followed smells and gusts that tossed my dress like their own blossom;

colors she'd drawn out of the ground

into light were the colors I learned. I ate sweet petunia stamens

and clover, and gravel from the driveway, till once she tipped

back on her tennis-shoes to make sense of something

I was saying, and saw dirt crusted at the corners of my lips.

In the dim house the baby slept and the drapes

were pulled tight as if it was never time to wake, but I understood

something could lift out of nothing, leaf curling up

from accident's seed.

MEMORY FROM THE FIRST HOUSE

DO YOU SPELL PUTTING P-U-T-T-I-N-G?—my little brother, squinting, feverish,

comes sleep-stumbling from our room, needing to know this—

DO YOU SPELL PUTTING P-U-T-T-I-N-G?—Putting what?

where?—weirdly precise, his sounding it out, but

panicky, as if his life depends on getting this question right. Putting—up, down?

Away, in its place? I'm the only one there to answer, thinking

what is he asking, though it's perfectly clear. The house had been so still,

unnaturally calm, like "Silent Night," as if something might happen, the tall

living room lamp shining its halo around the wide chair that I, the bigger kid,

stayed up in—but my brother was just supposed to sleep, Mom said

she'd given him aspirin, all I needed to do was stay awake—and he *had*

slept, everything peaceful with our parents out; just radio, then the sound off so I could

hear outside, inside, down the cellar, at the back, listen for the phone

but not answer, know when the car turned in. Now my brother's knocking along

the hall, eyes unfocused, out of his head, spitting this word that sounds like *HITTING*,

his sick body sensing too much quiet, the two of us left alone,

nothing wrong, no voice or hand raised, just this question—

what do I say—Yeah, P-U-T-T-I-N-G, and turn my brother back to the bedroom,

the question back inside his head, as if the silence might go on,

the front door locked, our parents' key, in some adult distraction far away from us, forgotten.

PRONGHORN

Shadows appeared earliest in patches of rough, steep
drop below the far east ridge, where the bluffs
fell off first, and antelope
fed together at evening on sage and grama tufts
that took less heat than the fields up top
or the lower bluffs stretching out to the river,
bleached grass bending east in wind, lifting up
sometimes then bending again like the fur
of bigger animals a hand might've just passed over.
Their elegant necks angled down as everything sloped
toward the river more than a mile across there,
full of sandbars whose shapes
the water slowly rearranged, so no map
ever stayed exact.

AFTER WILL'S NIGHT IN THE BARN

He said he didn't care. I leaned against the saddle
on its saw-horse, handing him the cheerios, asking why he'd knocked our cousin down
the night before, who was older than him, but littler, and a girl. His jaw pushed a frown
forward, eyes following angles of straw along the floor. Behind him, the tool-
bench gleamed its years of grease in hacks and scars. *Because she said Mom*
was part Indian. Said she couldn't be gone to any beauty pageant, and not just
because she's married. Horses snorting; swallows flittering dust
through the wide door's light-shaft rolled open—then beyond, up high, a shushing hum,
and at the door's gap more swallows shattering air—miles above the farmyard's square
of dirt, a jet. Willy running out to look for its trail dissolving, then gone, like we'd
never seen it. She'll come back if she can, I said.
I don't care anymore. I just want her to be somewhere.

SMALL NOTEBOOK

Your mom left it, Ellie, Aunt Ruthie said. But it must have been someone else's
before—the black leather cracked and fell apart a little bit
more each time I opened it to draw a bird inside, or yucca bloom, jack rabbit,
cartoon prairie dog with a lasso, more than once Uncle Ralph's horse, Bess.
The day Ruthie told me I should have it—and that she'd explain
when the time was right, but was sure our mom would be coming back
to the farm for Will and me—there was nothing in the notebook
but three rings that just fit my thumbs pulling them open, each a wishbone
snapped apart, then back in place, to hold the blank pages Ruthie gave me. First
thing I drew was the barn owl Uncle Ralph said brought good luck—worth its
screaming and waking us up in the night, better than poison for keeping rats
down. I drew all kinds of animals, then more than anything else, faces.
Not Ruthie or Ralph, or Lena or Annie, or Grandma, or even Will—lots
of faces, but no one I knew; young dark-haired women, some pretty, some not.

COUSINS: RIVER AND SKY

At dusk we climbed down the ravine to the twin cottonwoods
whose leaves turned and glistened like mica-flecks, like scales
of fish darting, reflecting the low moon, even like sails
in the harbors of far-off cities Lena claimed she'd
perform in one day, humming *East*
of the Sun as we waited at the river for
Kenny, the hired man's boy, who more
and more came after work, to tease
and teach us how to swim, how not to fight the currents, and how,
as we dried on the bank, to pick out constellations he said
moved and guided the birds
on their night-paths. *They come from stars and go*
back again, like the cattle, and the grass, and those coyotes we heard howling
out west of the yard last week.
                           I was first to swim on my own
and make him clap wet hands, but was sorry, since his hands
no longer had a reason to hold me then.

HEAVEN MAP

Eiffel Tower, cowboy, padlock and key, here and there a repeating butterfly:

figures snipped from old scraps of the little print dresses

and shirts and bibs Grandma and Ruthie sewed once. Ruthie's

said I've got a talent—*Call it originality*

if all the voters in Extension Club gave

first prize to that lop-sided cloud-quilt

you went and entered. Taut now in the oval frame on my lap: cut-out

images circled by deep blue rick-rack—*don't know who'd sleep under it, but you've*

got a knack all your own, Honey—long as you ain't wasting batting or fabric, you get

more done taking half the time than those cousins

of yours, tuning the radio, listening on the party line—

her words sharp, scrabbling at the chilly room's air, self-satisfied but

sidelong kind: little bothered bird settling on its bough again. Outside:

silence, layer of tulle across satin violet, what can't be known, refracted by night sky.

WILL'S HARMONICA

Blur of sundog at the horizon; cicadas whirring the air like static
before a dust storm. Cattle checked, and at the pasture-gate
two rattlesnakes crawling side by side, tails intertwined, looking straight
ahead, no hissing or rattling or striking one another, moving quick
across the dirt together, then gone into the grass—some
reckless dream of weave and balance we take with us
down to the river, till warm beer and dust tint the last
light pink. Curves of swallows trace their own messages, and behind them
the first pricks of stars link up—those we have the nerve to name and
others we can't make out. Even in dark, the lifting
and sinking cottonwood leaves above us keep flickering silver undersides, letting
go bits of fluff that tremble into the world like warbled notes, trusting wind.

LA FRAMBOISE ISLAND

Once when I was small I came far in, walking with my mother,
carrying a basket past the sign about French trappers who found
wild raspberries here, and scanning the ground,
thinking someone knew before then. Mom warning *watch for poison ivy.* Another
story as she and I turned back, our fingers stained red: it was here a bobcat
sprang and tore the jagged scar along Dad's belly. Nobody saw bobcats anymore—
it seemed a myth, made-up, drama and gore
to impress the dark-eyed girl my mother had been once, wearing his jacket
over her shoulders in a dim photo, leaning on his old Chevy. After the causeway
got built across from Pierre, once or twice I biked alone to the edge of the pines, but
never ventured in. Last evening, Kenny with a bag of sandwiches and a blanket,
pushing branches away, saying *something's out here you should see,*
 if you haven't all these years. Had Mom been shown those trees
opening on huge stones rolled to reflect the moon? Two-person island in the island's
distant sea.

II   CUT-OUT STARS

LIGHTNING MAP

Smell of moisture crossing the bluestem, riffling
my graduation tassel on the rear-view mirror; then sky
breaking to veins electric over the section lines,
and he speeds up, knowing it's already late for getting me
home. *Listen, my draft's high, and I got an offer—Clem Aronson*
needs a hired man up in Dewey County. Heavy air re-shattering; wide sheet
of tin warped back and forth over the land, loosening
all at once the rain that wouldn't come down in spring when we needed it.
He pulls over as the whole sky flashes white again. *Come*
with me. Clem's wife left him—they need a teacher for his and the two
neighbors' families. He says we can live in his old summer
kitchen that's a good ways from the house. I won't go
unless we can marry, Ellie. No stars now to see; only the promise
of his hand, map-threads marking each pulse.

SIOUX FALLS: VISITATION

1.

After a while nothing but the sound of asphalt humming under us, then
gradually outside Kenny's window a long pink line of dawn thickening,
glowing fluorescent as the panel-dials in front of us pale, and,
bending forward to watch the sky change, I move my hand from behind his neck—
along my forearm his curly hair grazing like light thrown off a sparkler—
word in cursive written on the air, then disappearing. Everything still, except
for tires' singing. A couple of cars pass going the other way, then only bitten black-top
and prairie; gradually full daylight shimmering grasses bent with the wind,
dew lifting off them—buffalo grass, needlegrass—a few yucca poking up,
unmoving—morning air raising a peregrine over some trailers circled around
a broken-off lamp pole, and below the bird a skinny dog runs out of a sway-backed
barn, tearing toward the road almost into it, yapping-nuts beside the truck, following
our dust a quarter-mile with its high-pitched scolding.
From the other direction an old man walking toward us along the shoulder—
for a second close enough we can see the long furrows in his face, his eyes not noticing
our pick-up coming up on him—concentrating instead on something beyond
us and the furious dog—
boots scuffing gravel, pace determined.

2.

Three colors of papers to fill out, pass under a bullet-proof window, then join
the long row of other people waiting to see if it's their prisoner's weekend
for visitation. Little girl bored, hopping back and forth across a painted white line
until a guard unbolts and shoves a rear door open yelling *STAY BEHIND
THE LINE OR YOU'LL BE TOLD TO LEAVE*—waking the girl's baby brother or sister on
her mother's shoulder—young mom saying to her daughter through the fussing *Watch in
that window at the back: they'll bring Daddy up from there.* Past

23

the metal detector, finally: a man already done, leaving, holding out to us a worn deck
of cards: *All 52 here—have fun*—the deck's edges soft as calfskin in my hand as
I look up to my father moving forward, face I haven't seen since I was ten, the letters hidden
in Aunt Ruthie's drawer until last spring—like watching the moon re-surface from behind
a cloud, body of shadow I know the wind will have to scatter again, the way pigeons
keep changing the old house, altering with feathers and droppings
the papers and magazines left on his desk from the night Mom said *Time to go.*
I remember hearing him tell once about his homesteader grandparents trying
to hang on to their place—how sometimes they'd ride over and set a lamp in
a window of the abandoned house down the road, just to feel there were still other
people out there. He comes straight toward me reaching out and hugs a long time, then
holds my chin until I don't know how to look back anymore, hearing him say
he'd pretty much given up; memory'd started leaving him alone too—*But look at you.*
We sit in chairs bolted to the floor, and I ask about Mom. *She wasn't staying away,*
no—if she could've, I know she'd have come for you kids. Kenny's hand on
my arm now. *As it is, she should've gone farther.—You know, sometimes in the middle*
of the night your voice wakes me just like when you were little, Ellie. Out along
the faint nerve-endings of roads that don't return messages, impulses settle in
the grasses that live on nearly nothing, need nearly nothing to go on bending in the wind
which strains and releases them, uncovering stars, hiding the stars again.

THAT'LL BE THE DAY (WHEN YOU SAY GOODBYE)

Will called up, Viet Nam

but crows understand—you know crows can count whether
everyone's gone home so they can roost again
watching for the one who's left and not come back
since sun and moon tell different stories where he's traveling

everyone's gone home so they can roost again
cries sent out to cancel crossed messages
since sun and moon tell different stories where he's traveling
moth-wings shadowing lanterns confused like the sea's

cries sent out to cancel crossed messages
restless as wheat under horsetail clouds
moth-wings shadowing lanterns confused like the sea's
to quiet the mind as stitching mends the day

restless as wheat under horsetail clouds
but crows understand—you know crows can count whether
to quiet the mind as stitching mends the day
watching for the one who's left and not come back

THE RIVER IN MARCH, ABOVE OAHE

Wind lifts the surface like a thousand wings rising,

as currents underneath follow their own dark

inclinations. Years of workers in hardhats

shifting the earth around with their machines,

flooding farms—whole villages—built the dam downstream

to span nearly a mile across, turbines

capturing the water's force, but not its secret of return

the geese follow generation after generation, tracing a dream

of origin. You search along the bank for smoothed stones

to skip—once, twice—five touches for one

before its drop—look for another worn flat enough to skim, then

sink too through the river, to a place beneath re-arranged and

re-arranged without end,

echoing some movement far above your outstretched hand.

SEVENTH-MONTH DREAM OR FIRST MEMORY

Blanket under trees it must have been; what throaty tune,
whose voice humming, what fabric, dress
fluid but velvety, or blanket on the grass below birds, restless
shadows of trees passing like clouds over a moon,
or a hand gliding across, movement before light
or touch, sound blurred to echo of float, heartbeat.

ANOTHER NIGHT OF HEAVY SNOW

Kenny took the baby out in her blanket, and she laughed at
the flakes whirling down—wet lace-touches, cold kisses on her face—
there and gone, like missing relatives'. He lay her back in the crib, saying *if it*
really starts to blow, we'll be searching at dawn to see what fences
drifted out, before sun burns through and melts the surface—
freezes over hard enough, them cattle'll walk right across. Any post-
top makes a shadow-compass with the sun, if you can find just
one pole uncovered—if you know that you're lost.

DREAM OF THE BABY'S WORD

How could summer darken every leaf on the few trees the baby
knew, then take them all at once in a gust—
"Da!" she said, which meant "Look!" or "That!" or "Many!" or maybe
"Red!" or "Down!"—it meant most
everything—her father lifting her up once more to touch
the bare branches.
But dream pulled the river till it rose above the bluffs, like I'd seen
once before, taking them one by one,
currents bright, dimmer, splitting open then concealing, rolling and
turning weedy waves—my own voice yelling out MARY!—KEN!—
couldn't make me heard to them, the echoes swallowed again and again—yet
no water touched me; only the wind, coughing, vacant.

SHADOW BOX

Streetlights fade to smoldering dawn; Mary still hanging on.
Even in this hospital two hours from home, wet smell of burning
finally finished won't leave us alone. And the parched wind,
constant, unstoppable, done with our house, snapping and
cracking the flag above the parking lot now, searches for something more
to empty out. *I'll tear it down,* said Clem, our landlord—my landlord—
what's left of it, when you're ready—build it again. How can he know that
in my mind I've taken the place apart
already, piece by charred piece, twice rejecting—what
half stands, a nothing, daylight sifting its bite of smoke—and the nothing held in it.

ALONG THE SINGED DRIVEWAY

Annie at the wheel, Ruthie holding on her lap a vase of pink
gladiolus for the cemetery, and Mary's fringed blanket—I'd forgotten to pack
it up again after our last visit to them—Mary starting to walk then, her hair finally
long enough to comb with the little silver comb that had been Ruthie's baby
gift, then pull into a ribbon. They've brought me clothes, some shoes and
underthings, things they know would've been burned or ruined
by the smoke. *Ellie, come back home with us*, they beg, *at least for a while*—but
I've got my work at the school, I tell them, need it because it
needs me—and Clem's said he wouldn't have wished anything like it before, but
having me in his house is a gift to the boys and him. I'll bring Mary's blanket
to bed with me tonight, pull it up close under the sheet in Clem's attic room
where everything worth saving from
my own house fits. Won't look at the mirror above the cabinet
left by Clem's wife; only at the silver comb that reflects it back, then out
the low half-window, to power-line lights beginning to blink
as dusk eases day behind the jagged windbreak.

FRAGMENTS AFTER FIRE

Thimble. Kenny's ring from the crumbled drawer. Blackened key Mary fumbled to turn

in its box at bedtime, to hear *How High the Moon*. Useless as fallen window-glass,

bedsprings, tools—ladder Kenny hadn't yet borrowed, to fasten

rods up on the roof, keep the house safe from lightning.

How to say it wasn't your fault, convince him

to say it for himself, inside the scorched walls that keep shimmering

and dissolving again

as if he might still be alive in them.

Two waking dreams repeat, one

contrary to the other, each filled with smoke

that rearranges: Mary lost already, but choking

in her sleep again, in the shadows of flames Kenny lifted her from—

he did—his own breath failing—coaxed her eyes open that night, and she woke, then

couldn't, after they closed again. *Time to sleep, Sweetheart*, he says. *Play the moon song again.*

WILL'S LETTER

In his pocket since Vinh-Long, he wrote at the end. Twisted, blurred from sweat and fungus rot

and cooking smoke laced with slow drifting smoke of huts

burned upriver, haze of rainbow-name chemicals his unit loaded there and

sprayed to sear the green tangle hiding VC. From call-sign

Hades, what was there to say to me—everything

ash around me, where everything was supposed to be fine.

That he'd pray? To gaudy jungle birds eyeing him from not-yet-bared

branches?—That he'll make it back—needs to find me here.

CLEM'S OLDER BOY, STIRRING

Soup of onions, carrots, potatoes, meat
falling apart, simmering, moving around
you never see the pieces all at one time
he says there's no point anymore in school

falling apart, simmering, moving around
he'll either farm or get drafted, only needs
he says there's no point anymore in school
to know what a hawk follows a coyote for

he'll either farm or get drafted, only needs
not much else, decent weather, a handshake
to know what a hawk follows a coyote for
maybe a few Johnny Cash tunes

not much else, decent weather, a handshake
why the government keeps shifting its missiles
maybe a few Johnny Cash tunes
who do they think they're fooling

why the government keeps shifting its missiles
radio predicting rain, men shot down
who do they think they're fooling
he's never been in trouble, never tempted

radio predicting rain, men shot down
their mother didn't want them enough to stay
he's never been in trouble, never tempted
calls once a month like he's in prison, or she is,

their mother didn't want them enough to stay
he dreamed of his parents laughing together
calls once a month like he's in prison, or she is,
over some joke he didn't understand

he dreamed of his parents laughing together
soup of onions, carrots, potatoes, meat
over some joke he didn't understand
you never see the pieces all at one time

PLAINS: STAR NAVIGATION

Today again the skinny Two Crow boy from up on the Moreau River
rode his stick into the schoolyard while the kids were playing
ball at recess. Looked as if he might've traveled all night, barefoot over
the hard-caked ground, arriving from another land. I heard Tommy saying
Wrong school!—then softer—*Here, take it.* Learned they'd given him a button to suck,
telling him it was candy. The big ones laughed when I scolded
them, and the little ones, glancing at Tom, then down at the dirt. Last week I took
the nervous new Agency-School teacher a quilt that our Green Grass Club had
sewn for welcome—welcomes, weddings, babies, sickness—my Mary's a pink
sunbonnet pattern, the last days she shivered in her burns—Kenny already gone—
Lena and Albert had come from New York to help watch over her, and finish picking
through what was left of the blackened house. Albert, washing his sliced hand,
told the story of his museum's smashed chandelier, and it took
hold of me as though it had been my nightmare. Only chandelier
I've seen's in the state capitol, but after Kenny fell dark,
then Mary, the sound of glass kept splintering in my ears, falling over and over
as if I were crossing a long blind hall barefoot, floor marked at every step with shards,
no place that wouldn't cut. Late today, I'd finished lesson plans, and the boy—Len—
was there at the gate again. His aunt lives down the road, he pointed. Might at first be hard,
I said, but if he wants to learn with us, he can. And help the rest of us learn.

RAIN FORECAST

to Kenny

Too late for the half-hearted half-rows of wheat;

they'll have to be plowed under. Soybeans might stand

if the clouds don't go round us again, wind taking along more of the land's

top layer from under our feet. Weather, war, old news—all I've got,

but meadowlarks clutch on the line, calling as if they've found

a reason to sing, as if the wires beneath them could

let me talk to you across the sky, and I'd

know what to say—toss me back the coins dropped in the Rio Grande

when you passed over? —or the River Seine, was it? —three of eight possible throws

we might've made together, all lost. Send a message from Hotel Corona Borealis—

was that the last stop on the train I missed when your sprung compass

fell and I leaned to find it, looked up and you were gone, God knows

where, if he does? No—whisper a further name—

farthest constellation you can see from there. Direction to look, before the storm.

III NIGHT SKY FREQUENCIES

TEACHER, WAKING

Dreams—I rarely

remember them anymore, but last night the bed

became the one Grandma and I used to share, and instead

of Grandma, the other person there with me

was the boy I heard from again last week, shy kid from

Timber Lake who wore a leg brace and used to sit at the back,

always drawing the others' faces. He'd sent an essay on silence and music;

hates his job at the bank, he said; asked if I thought he could write. Dream

turned the saggy old three-quarter bed to some kind of cage-like thing

that held us both, though separately—wired so we didn't actually

touch—and when his face came close to mine through the mesh, he

looked down, then back up at me, and I flinched, but kept staring.

Why should you be startled, he was asking. *Have you changed*

your mind? Is this not what you arranged?

MOON AND STARS QUESTION: EAGLE BUTTE

Strangest thing, picking up the mail—Merle

at the counter pointing out the fancy stamp and

New York postmark—not Lena's loose script, the seal

nothing she would make—and inside, three fluttering velvet birds hand-

cut, each set of wings beating differently, as if from Kenny a live valentine

had slipped into the mailbag amid dust and pokeweed pollen—addressed *Dear Mrs. Spiel,*

though—friend of Lena's, saying my shattered-night quilt on her guest bed *haunts my mind,*

has kept me wondering since the dinner at Albert and Lena's—would I feel

I could take a request, an order from a stranger who

can't from his distance barter, but insists on paying properly for my art. My Art!

My younger brother, Robert, an invalid, loves the phases of the moon

and every type of star, and would, I feel, sleep happier each night

under such rare imaginings as yours. With these swatches of cloth, I ask your advice,

and enclose a cheque, and my most sincere condolences.

NEW KID

Today at lunchtime Len Two Crow, running up from his aunt's trailer
over at the crossroads. Tommy had to ask first thing *Where's your*
stick you always ride? I looked sharp at Tom. Lately every day at recess
the kids have been racing, so inside I asked which animal would win first place
if they could have a race, and how. *Antelope! My horse! A leopard!—Can't name*
what don't live around here! Len was quiet, but held up the ruler I'd just given him
for arithmetic, and everyone stared. Finally, looking at no one, said *Ears on a mule deer*
are long as this here. They'll smell a coyote half a mile downwind, and their
eyes see front and side. Them big ears pick up a funny noise,
head lifts—they're gone. Ain't so fast as
antelope, once an antelope gets started, but hear twice as good. Mule deer,
they'll take off out of them shrubby draws quickest, sure.

CONSTELLATION QUILT THOUGHTS

Envelope from Lena. No letter, just a brochure—so like her—
from a show by her artist friend Joe. Not
paintings, though; little boxes, like rooms of dreams forgotten,
with round blue perches for birds that have flown, or
birds held in boxes, staring, whether content
in safety, or longing for the outside isn't clear. One a tiny
night hotel or distant blue palace—beads and butterflies
and a watch-spring spiral haunting it; another a window left
open, song of planetary sky, looking out or looking in like a wish
never told, yet known. Those blues of velvet
he sent me: where from or where to were they meant
to travel? Heaven quilt I might never finish.

DREAM: THE BOX MAKER AND HIS BROTHER

For a brother kept from the world, he'd make
a thousand different worlds, their keys bent from star-fragments
lifted out of peanut-dust circus tents,
plucked from ballerinas' dressing rooms or rain-flaked
birdhouses left vacant for finer places to fly to
than Bell Boulevard, Pearl White's pet pig
strolling on a leash there notwithstanding. Jacks tossed to follow across a sky in trains just big
enough for no adult-size hand to fit inside—or soap bubble, skirt-balloon
for traveling, Danish and apple pie in the basket or club-car,
warmed by opening an oven door at the hotel-restaurant destination whose mirror, if
tipped, reflects a briar-path humming the way to Shadow-Moon mountain, sifts
news of Houdini hanging from deck above the Sea of Tranquility, where
breathing underwater's easier if
first you slip the wheelchair, then snap the handcuffs off.

VOICES NOT HEARD IN MONTHS

I kept looking for signs they might return, though I knew

better. I knew the few dreams had been about me, not them. Still, I thought

swallows investigating the remains of the burned house might

be telling me something—and they were—though

not about looking back, not about going too. The seasons

darkening, flowers in the yard turning black and falling over

was impermanence without end, they said. And sometimes their

calls seemed to carry Mary's quick laugh—not as mockery, and not as

sympathy either; something else. They were gone when the river began at

the edges of the banks to freeze, day by day tightening further in

toward the center. I understood, as Ken would've—the water would melt again,

the swallows reappear—but our Mary—how could she know a thing like that?

LOST SOMEPLACE LIKE THIS

Rapid City, getting supplies

Someplace like this where it's winter too, but no city truck pours salt
for cars of people driving to work through snow—no one
works there, or feels the cold either, on the street where Mom slowly walks
a little ways, then stops, gazing into a shop window, avoiding
reflections of faces left behind, looking instead through the glass
for just the right fabric to make a dress—not for a baptism, not
for a naming-ceremony or a funeral—she's pointing, asking
which color, bending down beside my Mary, listening for what it is she wants.

FLURRIES

Cold air that has held for days its brittle grip

slowly opening, releasing a flake—something alive

out there, or like life. I stop my needle to watch: two—five—

over by the dark barn a universe whirls—sky relenting to tip

and let change fall in intricate bits

that startle against the window

then vanish to wait like dormant seeds below

the world of the visible. These days it's

hard to believe in green or even the tough pink

of thistle that crowded stalks before the cut,

before these iron months that seem to put

an end to change, blink

away memory of butterfly and swallow, stitch

them into quilt or dream, long nights I won't remember which.

A KNOCK

Vinnie Two Crow from the trailer at the school crossroads
has walked up through the snow, bringing a loaf
of pumpkin bread. Takes her big boots off
and sits for coffee. *Clem's always treated us good.*
—You up here had too much trouble. I open the bread,
and she asks about the quilt in my hoop. Stray
lightning quilt, charred toys quilt—I don't need to say
that. *If you want,* she says, *I brought some sage along. Good*
smoke might take away the bad, I told Clem out at the barn.
—If you got an old bowl or something to burn it in.

OLD DUGOUT

Will's birthday

From its mouth at the high edge of the ravine
we'd track clouds streaming bright
shadowed shapes, exact then changing, sending down light
or taking it back, air-glaciers rolling over our nowhere, bearing
underneath a restless flow of petals and tufts, quartz-glimmers,
uprooted bone splinters, tumbleweeds—loosened,
lifted weightless as
animal dreams, night-quivers, murmurs,
wind-scourings erasing our own scratches in the dirt
that said we'd been there, patient, bloomed
unseen as pasque-seeds scattered and grown, waiting, tuned
like cicadas, milkteeth, feathers tattered and gleaming, all the sky's trinkets.

WINTER, MAP OF THE WORLD BEFORE THE WAR

If I smoked, this would be my time to go behind

the building and say nothing of arithmetic, history, hands to oneself; puff

wasted breath into frozen air, watching the prairie, empty enough

already, cede grey drifts to sheeting white, heedless of kids or bell or line

of fence sinking. Through the window of the school, our map of the world tacked

across one wall: names of oceans, countries, rivers

in different scripts—bold and plain, italic—marking shapes already changing—lavenders

and pinks and greens charted, yet pale, blurred by snow, remote as facts.

CHRISTMAS PACKAGE: INDIGO PILLBOX

Beneath the lid, deep brown velvet interior,

winter twig of rhinestone-

buds resting there—and below the rim's lip, in

smallest type: *There is a pain—so utter—*

It swallows substance up. Turn it round

to read again, and the rhinestones glitter, little bough

of blinking eyes to take sorrow

in, hold it, keep it for their own.

STAR QUILT, AND STARFISH, SENT FROM A DISTANT PLACE, BALANCED AGAINST WINDOW GLASS

Thin as a needle, my need, like my work, piercing through
fabric-ripples, gathering stitch after stitch until
thimble turns it back at the pattern's curve, hardly a new
direction. I've understood well enough the dull
shore I was ferried to, no thought
of rowing further. Now these tiny stippled tentacles stir
up puzzlement, like gazing through ice to life underwater,
a vague shifting, not quite frozen through. Little alien listening for the murmur
geese follow in spring, as if you know that river-currents call to sky
and tell which way the ones gone already have traveled out of sight—
no, there's nothing to hear. Strange hand out of your element, don't whisper *try
noticing clouds pent up and opening*, as if they might
sift promise of some sea I can't believe in—wisp of snowmelt, dropped stitch,
caught breath, something beyond this.

CLOUD PASSING ABOVE THE PLAYGROUND

over the ones who keep getting taller, losing teeth, growing

hair, coming back with haircuts—the oldest sometimes testy now

—pimples appearing, no longer interested in much of anything—

not one is my child, but I can't hate them, hate their tracking in dirt

because mine isn't tracking any dirt in. Even now she'd only

be making small sentences, puzzling at letters; a cut

length of rope would be too hard to jump, the clock's meaning

too much yet to grasp—unless death's caught her up, passed her

through the grades in a rush, maybe taken her beyond me too, teacher straining

half the time for answers. I promised the kids: once the ground finally manages

to thaw, we'll plant zinnias beside the school. Even the big ones helped plan, saying

it's simple: bury the seeds on the south, water, fertilize; watch each day for change.

CAVE IMAGE

National Geographic

Torchlight would've wavered over
these antelopes' flight across pocky walls.
Then later, from under the dirt floor,
human bones surfacing—dusted, dated,
positions marked out like constellations—
and mingled with them, ancient seeds of plants that
couldn't have grown inside a cave, away from sun
—would've been gathered, bright flowers carried in
to cover the ones not coming out again.

GREEN-WINGED TEALS

to Mary

Even before the last snows have disappeared
they're back, their fiery heads and brilliant green eyepatches
skimming low over the water, dabbling again in the cattails and reeds,
rarely dipping all the way under for food, as they rarely did before,
restless, returned from some distant, different stand
of weeds, another river they need no name for.

LETTER AND CHEKHOV BOOK

Jacket wrapped tight, note snatched in a pocket,
hurrying through wind that sifts goldenrod the dusty mile
of cow-path to the lone tree at the neighbor's stock-
dam oasis. None of the words words that should thrill—
precise script, sentences from the actual world, far-
off artist sending of all things a book of Russian stories—but I need
cold air on my face. Ballet-program bookmark to boot: *The Fire
Bird*—not meant to mock, no—said he'd
thought I might have enjoyed it.—That is, were I acquainted
with his far planet. And send him, what—stalk of cheatgrass—in return?
Distance altered by watching the same stars. Something like that. *Faint
music from the sky at night, if you can tune it in.*
Meaning what? I won't re-read it. Beyond my boots, tangle of water-weed
grown to hide a maze of minnows fluttering underneath.

ARIADNE'S CROWN

Claw, bent U-magnet, grappling hook, hacksawed ring.
Torn nest, torn basket, broken circle of young girls dancing,
one fallen back to earth, a fool in love with a mortal, or just
a fool. Start at Arcturus and move on up to Izar, then east
a little—seven stars not terribly bright, except the single jewel
that haunts, lustrous rose from a wreath shriveled at sea's bottom, all
that's left of the snarl of nightbirds' worthless stories, ball of
thread unspooling that might've helped if you hadn't loved,
hadn't followed anyone to this island of memory unreliable, silent,
inscrutable as father, brother, lover, even friend, and as obstinate.

THANK YOU NOTE WORRIED OVER

—for the stories you sent, from farther away than you are, yet from

my own yard too—my landlord's—empty and full

of dust, like lost, losing, always, never changing Olenka's—name

I'd never heard of before—her nights like my nights, sleepless, dull

except for stars someone else might be watching, and Sadie, little black dog padding

in to rub along my leg after blank days of school, lesson plans, cooking then

for Clem and his boys, looking up in case clouds might gather from your direction, bring

a breath of moisture in the air. Sometimes, rarely, the night wind

will calm for a bit, buffalo grass and bug hum quieting all at once

like a conversation paused, something exchanged, perhaps

not meant to be noticed. Other times I startle, thinking someone's

knocked at the gate, as though I'd wakened from a long sleep.

STAR CURRENTS

Dark settling in; the combiners shut their machines down and amble over to smoke
in the yard's sudden quiet, joking, taking turns at the faucet. *Out in that oak
in the northeast quarter I saw a tinfoil star in a crow's nest, I swear.*
—*Must be one of them stars Ellie cut out at Christmas,* Clem's Jimmy pipes up. *If I wear
my red hat out by the road, there's one crow comes up close and acts like he knows it's
me. Like he likes me. Knows I ain't gonna steal his secret. What he does, he drops nuts
in the road for cars to crack open when they pass by: first he stopped while
I watched him, then he figured I wasn't gonna take his meal, and he called the whole
family over to get at it, lining up supper to be smashed.* The men laugh, and *No, ain't no
bad omen, crows,* says somebody. Next to the house blue asters have begun to
bloom like those stars the boys and I hung last winter, mirroring sky even in the dark, riffling
with wheat-scent and the higher currents that'll take us too, if fire or water, dust of spring
or some other season doesn't claim us first. We take what we need, we're taken
in turn; striped buttes and spires to the west were sea animals, then
sediments the wind keeps loosening and lifting. I learned to swim, but the hands
that baptized me are a different element now; my own hands strange to me as the wind.

ASYMMETRICAL STAR QUILT FOR ROBERT

whom I never met, but his and Joe's drawings helped me trust

that straight and curvy lines together could make the different sizes, alloys,

intensities of stars—copper-red, white, blue-black embroideries

surrounding explosions—like nests

jagged, swirling, some near-symmetrical as blossoms, some

leaf-shadowed, and a few overwhelmed by glo-bright

silver thread cancelling out whole sections of indigo velvet.

Below, on the opposite side, plain brown velvet lining,

buffalo fur turning its back to the pulsating lights above. Fifty-two

stars in fifty-three weeks, skipping one—last thing every evening,

listening to country on the radio, as if waiting for some reckoning

between confoundment and what's divine. Then it took two

more weeks to reach him. *We'd moved him and his model trains*

to my sister Elizabeth's on the island, where Mother is now,

where he could have his own room and watch the cardinals from his window.

Our friend Solomon said he had barely enough body left to keep a soul in.

On his bed now, a little damp with salt wind, your shimmering mapwork

of firmament, chart of bewilderments from the dark.

DREAM OF THE BOX MAKER'S DREAM

Again he's balanced on the front of the bike, and behind,

pedaling, his brother Robert who can't walk—no turning to look or understand how;

it's all downhill before them now along Voorhis Avenue—scents on the wind

familiar then gone as they ripple beneath the great bough

of the courthouse spruce, through shade passing the lilac row and out

into sun so blind he can't tell how fast they're headed

toward the valley—handlebars gripped beneath him as the mouth

of his brother howls a wordless echo—dread

that's never escaped before—voice almost no one's known beyond

their home, and sister Lizzie's, all the years of a life gone nowhere but

farther than actual wheels could take anyone,

unless now they can't brake at the tilt of the old road Robert

might not remember

bending so close on the curve above the river.

COMPASS BOX FROM JOE

Feather dropped inside the glass. Flown bird's tipped
a thimble over, sent the map
of moon geography rolling—chipped blue marble
slipped from some boy's pocket—thread and coil
and planet shifted to tune in ocean murmur,
memory no different from dream, whir of pleasure
or trouble or wanting out that traces faintest
change in frequency for the listener who darns a sock, or waits
to apply another coat of paint, or sleeps out
a night of thunderstorms rolling through, preparing to navigate.

HARMONICA, 45TH PARALLEL

Restless shadows along the porch-swing's slats—old truck rumbling

past, then fading out, its destination obscure

as the stars' births and oblivions above, blurred

by trillions of miles and mixed-up stories of who carried whom

to heaven, who abandoned, who cruelly punished whom. Now the moon's let

us into the Sea of Tranquility—how will we pay? *Have you travelled?*

Joe asked in one note. Mostly by thought, I might've replied. Round the world

where my brother, torn by shrapnel, doesn't write. Crickets, chain-squeak, car not

passing this time, turning up the driveway, making me stop the swing

and wrap my sweater tight, slip back into the house as headlights scan

the yard, then the engine shuts off. No sound of car-door, but some kind of tune,

long twin-wavering tones, not radio—and catching breath, I push open the screen.

SOUND AND QUIET

Glint of heat-lightning, murmurs off in the west;

then the air stills, settles itself, dusk pressing closer

to the river as currents twist

under shift of temperature, sorting whatever matter combs through their

tangle this evening. Half a mile up from milkweed and mud-scent,

not far back from the bluff's edge, two of us on the porch talking,

then talking less—family, war buddies not seen again, what to remember, claim, or let

go to cicada-sound in the windbreak that rises, takes over like the sea that covered everything

once, old music hardly noticed, lifting each night and dispersing it, until stars appear, a song

finishes, like waking.

from   A QUARTER TURN (1991)

RESTLESS AFTER SCHOOL

Nothing to do but scuff down
the graveyard road behind the playground,
past the name-stones lined up in rows
beneath their guardian pines,
on out into the long, low waves of plains
that dissolved time. We'd angle off
from fence and telephone line, through
ribbon-grass that closed behind as though
we'd never been, and drift toward the bluff
above the river-bend where the junked pick-up
moored with its load of locust-skeletons.
Stretched across the blistered hood, we let
our dresses catch the wind while clouds above
dimmed their pink to purple, then shadow-blue—
so slow, we listened to our own bones grow.

PUPPETS

Legs crossed, perched daintily
on the corner of her desk, Mrs. Twitchell
reads aloud from the Brittanica
a history of papier-maché,

her half-moon glasses aimed toward the page
and not the kids whose hands are shiny gray with
the novel mess of newsprint strips
and flour-water paste. At their age

the past is meaningless; here and now
absorbs them: wrapping goopy bands
around light bulbs brought from home.
But some envision little gowns

they'll sew to hide their hands beneath,
and a few already plan props
and headgear (crown; magician's wand and cap;
one girl, obsessed with Jackie Kennedy's grief,

will top her light bulb with a pillbox hat).
At the rear three boys slop paper on,
bored with puppets, racing one
another, scheming out of Mrs. Twit's earshot,

impatient for the paste to dry
so they can bash the inside glass to
rattle like maracas. Others smoothe
layer after layer hypnotically:

this one the way her father strokes her hair;
this other, turned aside, not once looking up,
as if it's himself he re-constructs
around the hollow core,

the way at home he pretends he has no real
body, that inside the fleshy sham
of face and butt and limbs that can be smacked anytime,
he's nothing, untouchable.

CAPTIVE

In the evening when my dad pulled his hat off
his forehead looked soft where it was usually covered,
above the line where the rough tan stopped.
Sometimes he took me along at dusk
in the pick-up, to close pasture gates
and check the cattle, and look out
across the wheat to the west, for the weather.
Maybe I'd ask a question about a bird, and he'd answer,
but he seemed alone, driving out,
bumping over the fields to a spot just to look beyond it.

On the road up to Uncle Norm's stood that old dying house
—it must be gone by this time—
the balcony was torn from the second story, and someone
could've walked right out into the air.
Almost every Sunday we rode past it, and I imagined
a young man held captive there
by the high grass and wind. Once when I asked,
Dad stopped the car so I could look in: some pigeons
flickered out; inside, between the boards of the walls,
thin cracks of light.

Whole afternoons while the horses sauntered and chewed
I'd scoot along the corral-rails, pretending the earth was fire,
trying to make it all the way around without touching ground.
Walking past the wind-break, I used to think
the rest of the world must look like that,
bleached dry and flat.

Wherever you turned
you could see the circle of horizon,
as the meadowlark repeated
four notes to the unbroken sky.

LEGACY

H. V. S., 1899–1986

So unlikely to have lasted
a lifetime on the prairie,
these turn-of-the-century toys
she left to me: an egg basket
for one egg only; the china doll
in calico I remember her calling Beulah;
and this glass pistol not ever broken
for the red and white pellet candies,
faded now, still trapped inside.

READING LATE

The heart wants what it wants—
or else it does not care—

So still. Not a cricket. In this heat
the trees around the house hold motionless
even at midnight. I trundle the electric fan,
little pool of wind, along with me
from room to room, and imagine Emily Dickinson
carrying a candle that defines her sphere
into a part of the house where she won't hear
her sister Vinnie start to snore.
Just now, while you're gone, I wouldn't
have to be reading her,
who closed herself in with her wild need
and the deprivation by which she meant
to know, wholly, her desire. No one ever
will figure out how much it was a wish
for someone in particular—Reverend Wadsworth,
maybe, her deep-voiced "Dusk Gem"—
and how much it was a longing that had no object
but oblivion, which allows no interruption.

A QUARTER TURN

It was a way to toy with the warning
against playing in the woods at evening:
they'd all coast down the three-block hill
with legs tucked and soles flat on the seats,
then jump off where the road ends abruptly
at the pines whose branches are so heavy, it seems
their own volition and not the wind that moves them.
Last night the first one tore in after his bike
and found a dead woman next to it:
breasts, thighs and face smeared with red, wrists
tied to a trunk with flowered shreds of her dress.
He stared, breathless, before flailing out,
and for the hour he might've spent with his family
or in front of the TV, he talked to police.
His friends will think of another game, but
tonight, after dinner, the boy comes up to his room
to watch from the window until there's nothing
beyond the streetlights' clear domain.

ORDINARY HEARTBREAK

She climbs easily onto the box
that seats her above the swivel chair, at adult
height, crosses her legs, left ankle over right,
and smoothes the plastic apron over her lap while
the beautician lifts her ponytail and remarks,
"Coarse as a horse's tail."

Then as though that's all there is to say,
the woman at once whacks off and tosses
its foot-and-a-half into the trash;
and the little girl who didn't want her hair cut
but long ago learned how not to say
what it is she wants,

who even at this minute can not quite grasp
her shock and grief, *is* getting her hair cut,
"for convenience," her mother put it—
the long waves gone that had been evidence
at night, when loosened from their clasp,
she might be secretly a princess.

Rather than cry out, she grips her own wrist
and looks to her mother in the mirror,
but her mother is too polite or too reserved or
too indifferent to notice any signal.
So the girl herself takes up indifference,
while hurt follows a hidden channel

to a place unknown to her, convinced
as she is that her own emotions
are not the ones her life depends on.
She shifts her gaze from her mother's face
back to the haircut now, so steadily, as if
this short-haired child she sees were someone else.

INSOMNIA

It's the ceaseless wind
off the prairie, blasting
grit into the window casings,
snapping one brittle weed against
the pane, rousing rattlesnakes—
blinded in this season
of shedding skins, they'll strike
at any vibration.

Try to lie without moving,
think nothing, sink,
follow the exposed poplar roots
that crowd to the lip
of the cistern's cool, cement lid:
within, broader than
your arm-span, three times deeper
than your height, the wet dark
of the slick-sided cylinder
does not admit wind
or snake. But you're too weak
to lift the lid alone.

FLOODED BREAKS

I remember drowsiness, the cloudy heat,
the familiar mixed smells of our sweat,
the pressure of my cheekbone against the front seat,
the sense of having forgotten a thing
you had just told me. Suddenly after hours
of talk and silence, dust and ragged plain,
we reached the Missouri's thick, unadorned curve:
rush of water looking muscular from above
and denser than the land there, which seemed
translucent for its lack of color,
as if the swallows plunging toward the cliff
might pass through it.
We drove on, but shining for a second below,
rising from the current where the bank had once been,
the tops of trees wavered, stripped and whitened.
More trees might appear in time
to line the river's new edge, but what we saw
was the starkness of a place forsaken, as if
our glimpse of it would be the last.

LATE MARCH

The geese are flying north along the river again,
searching the brittle fields for grain.
In the middle of the night I feel your hand on me,
and lie still.

I want to hear the geese, is all—
the dark calling for spring.
I want to go to the window and look for the moon,
thinking of no one.

The river breaks and then freezes, breaks and freezes,
trying to move.
What does it need from the birds
That follow it home?

BLACK AND WHITE SNAPSHOT

I'd been still before then, in the bath, watching
leaves flutter at the window's dull square, like
tickling, like ruffles on the swimsuit I wore
when I was little and Dad would carry me
on his back underwater. I began trailing
through the bath around my clean body
the dark washcloth that spread itself
gracefully as a jellyfish, animal
that stings what touches it.

My father posed me before those trees
in my starched dress, steadying my shoulders
between his hands. The shoulders
and white skirt keep me apart from the woods,
but look at the face, look at the curve
my neck makes toward the pine's textured trunk
that rises from the same decayed bed of ferns
I stand on and will return to,
alone, to lie down.

TO KEITH

(1954-1972)

In my dream you're waiting on the street,
idling outside the Lariat Café while I
count my tips and put the ketchups away—
you're leaning out of that
jacked-up pink Chevy we'd bolt town in
to tune in the rock from Oklahoma City
and skim along moon-dim back roads,
going nowhere. You raise your arm to me,
the one with the hand cut off, though that's not
the way you did it. You pulled the Chevy
into the YOU-WASH-IT after school,
rolled both hinged doors down to the concrete
and slid back in behind the wheel,
radio up, motor roaring.
But in the dream you're still waiting for me,
your old girlfriend, the one
you gave your diaries to that day
—and I didn't ask why, though we weren't
going together anymore; I didn't ask,
didn't even look before
I stuffed them in my locker at lunch;
I liked being the keeper of feelings,
being needed but not touched.

LEAVING DAKOTA

Do the prairie-winters breed this silence
we've learned to need?
There must be prairies in Sweden.
The Nystroms pressed into America
two thousand miles for empty land,

and not an inch south. When the old man died,
Great Grandma traveled back
to Sweden to find his brother,
returned with him her second husband
to the same sod-backed house.

Five months waiting out
ice-winds held off by no hills, no trees,
as the miles between farms increase;
the stark intimacy of one room
survived with silence and fire.

So it comes from weather, this restraint?
Into our moment of goodbye, your broad face
looming, Father, the lines in your lips,
the gray-green eyes, suddenly;
our quick, shaking kiss.

WORDLESS HOUR

Look at the lilac, vivid and dying
in the honeysuckle's clench,
whose scent is sweeter yet.
—And the shadows they make together,
darkest in this heavy glare, this weight,
almost like rain on the air, although
the sky is clear. These things I say
to nobody, tilting my head to fasten
my earring, while you wait beside the car
in the long rectangular beam the window
throws like a spotlight into the evening.
Somehow it makes you vaguer, though:
jacket flapping before the trees in motion,
branches in the dusk at your back
entangling and dissolving.

PARTING

Nothing could have made it less abrupt—
not the next taxi instead, not a longer hug,
a placid rather than a drizzly sky;
nothing would have made you cry before
I was in, telling the driver where to take me,
and you loaded in my bag and closed the door
carefully, holding on an extra second
to the wet handle, then letting go

while through the streaked back window
I watched as long as possible
your shaking head, your one hand raised to me;
then watched the rainy blossoms
shaking on the trees; and then, beneath the trees,
other people on the streets—
some hurrying, some not; all of them,
all of them remote.

THE DREAM OF BURNING

—Villa of the Mysteries, Pompeii

They were not burned, but suffocated
by the time all color finally flared
beneath the black cloud and faded.
Yet this buried room—in blood-red,
gold, and purple—preserved the dream of burning,
dance of the body's furious wish,
arc of the whip snapped against itself.
Like water splashed and arrested,
figures lean their heads together, and whirl,
and bend for the lash of initiation.
A satyr stares at the augury inside a bowl;
a stiff-shouldered, naked boy— the youngest—
keeps his eyes on the page of some sacred text;
while the rest gaze from scene to scene at one another,
except for the veiled one alone in her corner by the door,
who seems rapt in the whole drama before her.
She—even more than Dionysius, who sprawls,
spent, in the center panel—she presides.
Or is she also the one with cymbals?
Or flinging her shawl up in alarm?
Or arranging her hair before a mirror,
preparing for what comes when, closing eyes,
not only thought but even the body is forgotten?

POEM FOR A BAD HEART

In Florence in winter those stone
churches are colder than the streets;
does the old caretaker-priest,
wrapped in his cassock and muffler,
sit this morning in the Santa Maria del Carmine,
shifting his chair hour by hour
with the light from the south window,
attentive for off-season tourists who call
"Massacio?" with its comic echo?
Is he pointing them another time to the far front,
right of the altar, the Brancacci Chapel,
where Saint Peter still draws
the coin from the fish's mouth behind
scaffolds and nets and torn canvas flaps,
so that to see it they have to lean
uncomfortably left, and press
their faces against a pipe?
And will they have the patience after this,
despite travelers' weariness or a spat over breakfast,
to listen to the old man's apology,
his entreaty to return when the work
is finished, his wish that his own heart last
through the final restoration? Has anyone
known those Massacios as he has,
the day-by-day dimming of Adam and Eve
as they howl out of Eden?
How will they finally look to him,
redeemed?

JANUARY HALF-LIGHT

Sunless, shadowless dream-time,
ironing shirts by the window,
listening to the stereo play again

"My Foolish Heart" in Bill Evans'
drawn-out, plaintive alteration
that makes the notes mean

for once what they always wanted to.
Across the valley that I watched you
trudge down early in the afternoon

parasol pines sway as if the glassy sky
were almost water-density,
like half-lit smoke in a jazz club

where people across the room
seem to move weightlessly,
lifted and tipped by old mute wishes

the music returns them to.
The piano drifts, dips; the drums
tump on their own for a bit; someone

steps in from the forgotten cold
and stamps his boots. Steam rises
as I lift the iron and set it

on its end in sudden quiet,

turning to see if it's you there again,

in your damp coat.

TO JANNY

(1953-1984)

The highway stills a minute;
I can hear leaves simmering
in the wet heat, and, posed twice
before another truck shudders past,

the old question of the bob-white
—one note hesitant, one perplexed—
we used to imitate.
Nothing moves except the traffic

and a river-elm dragging its branches
a few inches across the grass
like a girl's long hair when the tire-swing
has come to rest and she tips her head far back.

HER WALK ALONG THE CREEK

I hate the smell. Always
I'll hate it. Pine: not woods,
but that farm-grubby bathroom.
The coarse, grease-cutting soap my uncle
made me use when he'd finished inside me.
I don't know how we never were missed
by anyone; don't know how to care
that someone must've done a thing
like it to him.

What hurts most, what
is nearly or completely forgotten—
does it have to be turned
into further hurt instead of something
new, something not wrong,
like these ferns uncurling from rot
on the caved-in log? I take
another step: the quick, faint
shock of walking through a spider web.

COTTAGE ABOVE THE HARBOR

Now, at dawn, back from the dock's brink
stumps a small blond boy with a bucket,
singing something to himself.
How did he first get to the end of the dock
without my seeing him walk out? And who
lets him wander here at this hour alone?

As though waiting myself for his return, I've
been pacing the porch-boards from corner to corner,
watching the shadowed masts tip back and forth
like indecisive compass needles, while inside
my husband sleeps on with his hand under his face,
trying to answer his separate restlessness.

I wish the boy would not turn left or right
when he steps on to the road, but come
straight ahead, singing his song
up to this house to steady us, as easily as
he steadies his bucket of unknown contents.
With one hand he does it.

AT OCRACOKE

This silver light could dissolve everything
into one substance. Already the borders
of sand and ocean and air are unclear,
and people down the beach glitter
and shift like bluish chips of jewels
washed in from some old shipwreck
and left to mix with the seaweed strips.

Even what's up close wears the blueness
of distance: a styrofoam cup; these half-sunk
slivers of fishbones; your dingy running shoes
dangling from the hand that swings, familiar,
beside me. We walk, letting the cold foam
rush about our ankles and recede,
letting the waves take what talk might be

between us now, as though they could form
an answer, while we split our attention
between the curving, fading line of shore
we might like to follow forever
and the beautiful broken shells
dropped at our feet by the water,
imperfect, each becoming something else.

LYING AT PANCAKE FALLS

Perfect spot, with the perfect slight
indentations. Hips, breasts, elbows, cheekbone
—my whole weight pressing into this hot
flat stone would've caused no suffering
and felt none, had it lain these years
just another stone slope,
sunlight and water braiding over it.
Across the layers of rock below,
strands of creek separate, then recompose
their rivulet—an accident, like the one black
igneous streak through granite
outside the old Dakota Museum, with its
stuffed buffalo, gas-mask from World War Two,
skull discovered caging the flint head of an arrow.
Out front, unmarked, half-sunk in the grass
by the parking lot, lodged the prayer rock:
smoother than this stone, leveled,
made beautiful by its long, grinding journey
beneath the glacier. Long before my visits
after school, the Lakota had worn into it
the half-inch deep impression of a hand
that drew your own hand down to fit
where thousands like and unlike it had been
cradled by absolving, indifferent stone.

AFTER THE SERVICE

Who knows if Grandma Hazel believed
in any sort of god beyond the whims
of dust devils and thunderheads?
She went to church when taken: weddings,
funerals, obligations. But Mom, who seems
suddenly frailer, wearing her mother's
cloudy opal ring—Mom lived more years

in town: I could tell as a kid that she
believed she should believe. That did her
more harm than good, as far as I could see,
but each week I'd walk myself to Sunday school
with my starched dress rocking, wanting
to be the little savior of the family,
to memorize right answers for everybody.

Tonight we talk late at the kitchen table,
Mom and I, neither of us saying we have
no hope to sleep. Now and then
her left hand turns the worn ring that must
be large for her. Now and then I put
my arm around her, tiny woman,
last shield against the questions.

from   TORN SKY   (2003)

LISTENING IN BED TO YOU READING *SWANN'S WAY* ALOUD

A dimmed coach-car carries me
along the curving rails

through violet-shadowed
swells of snow where

there are no signs,
no names; at the window

only the undulating white,
frame after frame unreeling

this question of time,
your voice speaking low

in sentences that throw
reflections, like those

at the drive-in movies
I was taken to in my pajamas,

and where I watched not the pictures
on the screen, but the shifting lights

as they passed over car hoods,
fanning through the dust-hung dark,

above the raspy noise
of the speaker-boxes

that could have been, say,
The Bridge on the River Kwai—

shouts, explosions, a flock
of mouths whistling,

all this something different from what
my parents in the front seat

heard and saw, and conjuring exactly
what I knew this dream to be:

the secrets of all brilliance
and sorrow flickering up

like swifts into the night sky.

IN ITS PLACE

i.

my father hasn't met
the new neighbors yet
he's measuring to see if
the tree whose branch tore off
last night in the windstorm
is their poplar or his own
theirs he decides and gathers
what fell from his trees
dumps it in the pickup
but not that heavy sucker
it's theirs he leaves it
heads inside forgetting his golf game
and the buddy waiting for him
he's going to watch out
the window wait and see what
kind of goddamned people will
leave their trash on his property
but he's not going
to be the one to speak

ii.

one of these days his brothers
and he have got to figure out how
on earth they're going to divide
their old man's land up
three decades Dad's managed

the business kept the home place
more than once from going belly-up
last week he drove out to Uncle Norm's
with Case parts and helped replace
the belt on the irrigation pump
they talked about crops and prices
till Dad started in about
getting a count of the chickens
certain some were missing
when he left
Norm got in his truck followed
him all the way back home
keeping just out of sight behind
sixty years since they had
any chickens on any farm

iii.

he reads now
he never read before
reads in his plaid TV chair
face set like he might be at
the tractor's wheel making passes
across an uncultivated field
page after page about the parts
of his life he once thought
just as well forgotten
about the Depression and Pearl
Harbor but also golf and Arnold Palmer
who was born the same year

he was came from nowhere
and nothing did everything with such
back-asswards will and never
was meant to amount to much

iv.

visiting Virginia visiting anywhere
makes him uneasy and now
it's snowing we're stuck inside
he keeps getting up from
our card game to look out the window
it's not so much restlessness though
as a kind of reluctant marveling
at the lack of wind
snow is a thing he knows
has shoveled frightened horses
out of tunneled through a whole day
from house to barn and blocked
from his face when after a week and
no sign he plowed through his Uncle
Albert's drifted-over road to find all
sixty cattle frozen in the windbreak
Albert in the tub wrapped in every
blanket he had alive but empty-eyed
he never spoke again
Dad lives in town now but even so
when it snows you don't see
the neighbors' place or anything
but a wild derangement of wind and ice
and air yet here on our deck

big fairy-tale flakes
falling straight down piling eight
inches straight up atop
the birdfeeder birds will find
the seed you can look out across
the even white to lights on in
the next house and the house
after that and everything seems
to be in its place

GRANDDAD

When supper was over he'd pull
the little pouch and bundle
of papers out of his pocket,
then peel free one white sheet
to fold into a tiny pair of wings across
his scarred left palm that twisted where once
the whole hand had torn off in a threshing machine.
With the right he'd loosen the drawstring,
tap a narrow line of flakes along the crease. Roll the wings
together then—little cylinder—and pinch. Lick the seam.
Cracked lips puckered to the paper as he struck a flame
and puffed it into swirls hovering, then
fading above his head. Sometimes
he'd let me snug the string tight again.

HOMESTEADERS

After a while you'd stop talking
about the Old Country or the East—
like as not, the past went back

to somebody running from something,
needing to forget. This place
held no reminders, no blame.

Shadows of clouds stealing
across the plains, visible
from miles away, could be symbols

of nothing but the clouds themselves:
darkened only bunch grass,
buffalo grass, and tumbleweed,

then left them alone again.
Along the riverbed cottonwoods
flashing silver under-leaves in the wind—

what could they be signaling?
If you made it here you had
a hundred sixty vacant acres

to prove up, then claim for good; nobody
watching, only prairie larks
afloat like dust in bottomless sky.

TOLL

How many Indians from the Missouri tribes died of smallpox… can hardly be estimated. Possibly one hundred thousand.

-Evan S. Connell, *Son of the Morning Star*

No, Sven—I couldn't part with it—
Mama had woven that blanket when she
sang me lullabies, and on the boat wrapped
herself inside its tulip-patterned blues
to ease the shivering and itching,
till the captain sent her bound in canvas
down through the waves. I hid it then.
It's all I have left, Sven—

        —It's all, yes, he hissed
*—we have to keep the food and tools,
and these people want what they haven't
seen before, they want pretty things,
and I won't be giving you to them.* Pretty
was a word I'd lost on the journey—
        My face—
Mama would sob into the blanket,
and I was glad we had no mirror on the passage.

Their chests glistened above the switchgrass
outside the wagon; dark fists gripped
the ponies' manes, and I couldn't think
of those hands taking back to their tipis
what I had saved of her. For the first time

since I'd locked it, I lifted the pine trunk-lid
back on its hinges: *Live,* I heard
Mama whisper, *let them have it.*

REGARDLESS OF THE FINAL SCORE

No matter which side was more
battered and mud-smeared,
at Homecoming we cheered for game's end,
when the king and queen appeared
in eagle feathers and buck-skin:
hundreds of palms drumming bleachers
as the royal pair lifted a torch-pole,
and flames snapped along gasoline-soaked
rags wrapping the goalposts.
We left them to burn, weaving
the snake dance down Main Street then—
a school of white kids flinging ourselves
along the dark, as if some current we couldn't
understand passed through us, like the impulse
of the showhorse Sitting Bull had accepted
from Buffalo Bill: when Lakota followers
crossed police about to arrest the old chief,
the rattled animal raised one hoof
as it had been taught, fluttered
its mane and spun to pace out
all the tricks it knew began with gunshot.

KEITH'S DREAM

My father ran and fell down and the blood came
out of his mouth, and then a soldier put his
gun up to my white pony's nose and shot him,
and then I ran and a policeman got me.
                    –Herbert Zitcalazi
                    survivor, Wounded Knee, 1890

Keith's brother had a state-house job—
never told anyone they were Indian. Would've
killed Keith if he'd known the things
he told me, but no one was keeping track
of Keith much those last months.
After school, after wrestling practice,
after his shift at the D & E Diner
where he and the gory-aproned cook threw
knives past each others' ears in the wee hours
when the cook would start in again
calling him Little Brain, Shitting Bull—
around four he'd come to the window
to wake me, and we'd roll away across
the dark gravel, his muscles tensing
as he picked up speed out of town, headlights
tearing through grain dust, the two of us
imagining who we might be someplace else.
Once above the river he pulled off, leaned
his head against the gritty seat, asked if
I'd sleep awhile there in the car with him,
so he might not have the dream
of the boy playing on the pony when

the shooting began, or hear again the words
his grandfather used to say to him—
They'll all come back one night—
the ghost shirts will bring them,
and the pieces of buffalo will bring
the buffalo, the land will be the way
it was again. We'll see that night
who the ghosts are. Don't let yourself
get any more white.

We didn't sleep, we watched the light
creep along bluffs and buttes
puckering the tufted land above the river,
the place he said it would first
be renewed. We watched swallows lift
from below the bank. His hands were fists.

in memoriam, K.E.O.

108

FOUR SHEETS CUT OUT

We could see a great distance in every direction ... high smooth prairies
and some fine bottom ... gangs of buffalo at a considerable distance .... We
went the highest course to the River of Little Children... proceeded on
and struck our old track and returned back to the pirogue about sunset ...
had a little rain this evening....

25 August 1804, *Journal of John Ordway*
Sergeant Major, Lewis and Clark's Corps of Discovery

Four sheets ... have been cut out ... and only the stubs remain.
Gary E. Moulton, Editor
The Journals of the Lewis & Clark Expedition:
Vol. 9, The Journals of John Ordway

25 August 1804: After Floyd

Captain Lewis awake also. We set
the prairie on fire as a signal to the Sioux
to come to the river. Nothing yet
but silence, and now and then low flute-
like notes from the yellow-throated bird close by
every night since Sergeant Floyd's burial—
small meadow-skimmer of some kind; we haven't tried
to name it yet. No one speaks of Floyd; on the map we will
carry back, his bluff is fixed; one of us will have to show
his people where we lit a flame on the mound
before shoveling, and took from his pocket the tow-
hair-bracelet that we found
to bring back to them. After this, no more lashings in the dust,
I pray; the captains see how punishment divides us.

28 September 1804: Past Bad-Humored Island

High wind from southwest. Whitehouse has taken watch. Myself dead-
exhausted, the pirogue still leaking a bit from its swing round with the current into
the barge. Bows strung along the banks, spears—Lakota, who
said we were bad medicine, seized our boat-cable, then begged us not to go ahead.
Today again the chief took the line, testing our nerve. Wind coming over in
gusts and rasps like throat-yowls of their dances, moccasins shifting the dirt,
pipe-smoke, tambourines rattling antelope-hoofs, the last tobacco-carrot
given by the captains not enough: drums thrown to the fire. Tonight on
our boat anchored at the middle of the river
one chief sleeps with us. Captains remind him
he has promised to send his Omaha prisoners
back to their nation. No telling his intent.
Two elk swim
close by the boat in strong current.

4 October 1804: After Watch

As if flung down, men who have pulled all day
toward the unknown lie strewn beyond
sleep, floating their dreams over this land
of no hills, no trees, nothing but the laughing bay
of crooked-backed wolf-dogs, memory of bones—fish
skeleton longer than our keelboat knocking at
the cutbank. The river our own blood now, yet we pump against it
each day, against the heart we don't know except as wish,
as hope. Wind across these foreheads like a hand; lightning jolt
in the west; whiff of rain-pocks on dust like the smell of Betsy's

mother's Bible—she had opened it
to Corinthians, *we shall not all sleep, but we*
shall all be changed—shock of prairie-grass blown wet across
my face like unwept tears asking *will you wake from this?*

31 August 1806: Vision, Return

Not one of us raised a hand or more than glanced
as we rowed past—Black Buffalo hooting after us,
lifting his rifle over his horse,
above the bank where the scalp-dance
shadows leered two years before.
Only the captain's insult shot back across
the giddy current, as our parting this last
hostile place drove the oars
faster downriver than the river
itself could tumble toward the Omaha and home. Then
laughter; Frazier and Cruzatte began to sing; I shivered
and looked up: above us all a tearing open of sky, sudden
as the temple veil—sheets of arrowhead swallows shearing down,
then swerving past us to their riddled cliff. Then gone.

THIEVES

In any big city my father made
a point of knowing how to find skid row
and drive us slowly through.
My mother would rattle the map and complain
and reach to lock car doors, while my brother
pressed against his window, and I slid down
further in my seat, embarrassed by the solemn
exaggeration in my father's voice. Burnt-out
neon signs. Bums the color of pavement.
Poor sons-of-bitches, he'd always say.
Luck will rob you a thousand ways.
It was thirty years before I'd see
the picture of him, age five, in government-
issue overalls, posed with his brothers
by the crank Ford, under a dust-eclipsed sun.
Cropless seasons were all they'd seen,
till that spring a thunderhead opened over them,
coaxing forty acres of decent corn. For weeks
they measured the stalks that climbed the air
until the morning an eerier sun-darkening
clouded up from the south:
grasshoppers searching out any green spot.
In a matter of hours the corn devoured—
then fenceposts, window-curtains,
paint straight off the house; hoppers plugging
the old Ford's radiator, clogging calves' mouths
and nostrils till the animals collapsed.
Nothing left, and still

they whirred down in waves, piling up
in shady corners a foot and deeper.
After a day you could step out in the yard
without getting smacked and tobacco-stained
by the hail of them, but the place you knew
was gone. Cousins, neighbors gone soon after.
Grandpa packing up to find town-work.
Where? For how long?

Once, on vacation in New Orleans, even Mom
was too hot to keep the windows rolled up
on our detour. We felt as gritty as folks
on the street anyhow, and this section of town
wasn't the colorless smear he usually took us to:
vendors juggled oranges, and tourist-carriages
clipped through, the horses sporting straw hats
that swayed through jazz curling out
of open doors, intricate as the lacy
iron railings wound with flowers above us.
And to our amazement Dad was pulling over,
beckoning to an old guy with a cardboard sign:
TOURS. FIVE DOLLARS. A whiff
of licorice as he crawled in back with us
and talked Dad toward the cemetery
where ornate graves were stacked
above ground to keep the sea
from rising up and separating families.
Here it wasn't dust, but water
that had threatened—even the dead.
Brad and I scuffed in and out of shadows,

following lizards that flashed and vanished,

as Dad read the tiers of names to himself.

Trouble was, the old fellow warned,

sometimes thieves broke into these graves,

looking for whatever they could

take off the bodies, so even if

a name showed up here, the soul might be adrift.

LEUKEMIA

My mother's given up on her dream
of a brand-new house. *What's wrong
with what we've got,* my father doesn't
say, exactly. "Go ahead" is what he says,
not *I built this one myself, it's where
we've lived what life we can recall—
what would I do in a big new place
with nothing familiar?* Nor can she say
It would help me. And neither will admit
I'm too weary for this argument.
It's a slow leukemia she's fending off—
she could have years, and we take them
as given, rather than track this passing one
for the shadow of when she may be gone.
So, gradually she's patching new house in
over old. My father wakes disoriented under
his ceiling-fan birthday gift; bangs a hip
on the ornate-handled chest of drawers at night.
New gleaming sink in the bathroom with no
encoded blooms of rust, and above, open wings
of a triple-lighted, three-way mirror—
she says she wants for once to see the back
of her own head.—Where her own mother must
have cupped a hand sometimes, saying *Darling.*

SNOW

for Brad

Fifteen below and wind at sixty,
no way to get the feeder to the cattle;
they'll have to tough it out or not
till the gusting dies down—
if they weren't the neighbor's herd left
in your care you'd forget them—
no, they'd be gone, sold for the pleading
or the settlement, like everything.
You think of cutting the motor off to sit
in the tractor cab awhile, radio songs slowly
fading out as they suck the battery dry,
white nonsense scattering at the windshield
like bits of wreckage hypnotizing
till some kind of sleep comes on—
no sleeping in the house, the bedroom closed,
the kids' rooms too, you only go
to the couch and listen to television voices
calling as if to a lifeboat they don't
know anything about; once in a while the
answering machine—not her, just
your mother or sister, worried, trying to
coax you to the phone, draw you out,
but you're too tired to tell them there's
nothing left here to worry about:
if the gusting doesn't die down soon
the cold will finish all of it.

TWISTING VINES

My mother bought a dress once and my dad
said it looked like curtains. Nothing if not honest,
nothing much but me to his name, doing his best
about the trike and baby pool, new triple-speed
living-room fan, her just-landed job as a typist
while her mother babysat. There must
have been some wedding, or National Guard
occasion—James-Dean handsome he was,
even in eagle-crest hat, glare-polished shoes—
but the dress went right back in its creased
paper bag, unused. She had modeled it for me first
though, gazing over each shoulder to the longest
mirror before he got home, smeared and hot
from painting houses. *How does it look, hon?*—
that dress I remember more than any other,
off a rack at London's, our two-block downtown's
only clothes store. *Scoop-necked,* she called it,
for summer. Cap-sleeved. White, with a pattern of
little twisting green vines. I touched the satin piping
that showed off her collarbone, tiny waistline.
Made her look like a full grown fairy out of my book.
Those days she still sang when she sifted flour, folded
laundry plucked off the line by the morning glories
and tulips—"Tammy's in Love", "Blue Moon",
"My Buddy." Never again got herself
what she wished for, if she knew.

HALF TIME, OGLALA HIGH, 1970

Waiting in green-and-white pleats
in the ladies' room,
we were starting to think
this game didn't need us. Our team
would clobber them, then get ushered
from locker room to bus;
we'd turn back with Pam's mom
and the beaten Reservation crowd:
front entrance, dim parking lot,
dimmer broken-lighted streets.
No telling now what this chopped,
low talk in the dim bathroom was—

bead-shirted girls with
great cheekbones slouched
or sat on the sinks, looking
us over and smoking, some
swinging the high moccasins
we'd been told they liked
to hide their switchblades in.
Pam and Judy and I fixed eyes
on the stall-doors in front of us
that more smoke curled above.
Toni picked at her fingernails,
fuming for us to hurry,

but Sherry, whose platinum braid
glimmered like a crazy

challenge in there, squeezed over
to the cracked mirror by the door.
She dug the pink brush
out of her shoulder-bag,
and I groaned, but Pam shrugged:
let her keep the stares over there—
even the two Oglala white girls,
aloof in a corner till now, glared
as she pulled the ribbon out
and shook loose the luminous hair

that had got us free rides
from the carnies last summer.
Sherry kept right on primping
when the gaunt girl in cowboy boots
snorted, pointing her cigarette
in my direction: my sneakers—
the little yarn pom-poms I'd laced in—
made her hiss what sounded like
ought to take their white legs off.
Nowhere else to pee.
I read obscenities scraped
into the dented metal in front of me,

listening for the buzzer and the boys
back dribbling, knowing these girls
weren't there for the game, but to take
our measure—our blue-shadowed eyes

and pearl earrings, our perky routines.
How could it have come as a surprise
when Sherry leaned, lifted
another handful of hair to brush,
and a fringed arm flashed, jagged
it off, then was gone before the scream?

FRIEDA'S PLAN

Yankton State Hospital, 1973

Snow's vanishing above the condemned
tunnels, where patients sometimes
sneak down to do it. Or smoke
their smuggled weed. A little
basement heat still leaks through.
The ones sleepwalking without coats
from building to building don't
even know the tunnels are under them.
Maybe spring will stop their coughing,
and I might have a chance
to sleep, she writes in her
assigned journal, conjuring
plausible thoughts, since
hearing voices is what got her here.
—She pulled out too soon on Jake,
whose quick grip would've shut her up.
Well, plenty on the Rez listen
to voices, but not so many rip through
a state cop's cheek with his own pen.
—No time done for the shit *he* was trying.
She could damn well walk down
the Interstate in December if
she wanted, forget who told her to,
or where she was headed before this
detour.—Like a dream of getting
loaded up all over again and locked
in the cinder-block Indian School,

where they cut off and burned
the little medicine pouch
her mother had made to protect her.
Fine. She's always had her own
medicine. Doesn't write that down.
Stopped talking after the trooper,
but what she knows, she knows. Like
why the lame kid who tends the birdfeeder
did what he did to his dad's skull
with a claw hammer. Who those birds
are really. And that the new so-called
teacher here drives home in her faded
jeans and crooked jaw to get
beat up on after supper. She knows too,
can see clearly, as if she's watching it,
that one of these longer evenings coming
the teacher in her sweetest tone
will arrange to take poor Tom Smith home
in her red car for supper. Her project:
Tom hunched at the next desk there,
who's been on the locked ward for fourteen
years, and who's rewinding yet again
the crackling story of "Stone Soup"
he can't get enough of—digs it out
every single day to play. *All the people*
in the village hid away their food
as soon as the beggar appeared.
What can Tom Smith have done
too long ago for anyone including him
to remember? *But when they heard*

he could make soup from a stone,
they opened their doors again. One by one
they brought out what he knew
was waiting for him. Every time
the beggar pulls off his trick,
Tom rasps that laugh she's let scrape
inside of her. Fine. She knows
she went deeper into him; now he won't
go anyplace she doesn't go. Below the dripping
windows buried passageways to nowhere show
only for this morning: a ring of broken
links crossed by cottonwood shadows.
By afternoon the patterns in the trampled snow
will fade to nothing, but an evening
is coming when Tom Smith will fold
himself into the front of the red Subaru, and
Frieda will slide in back. No need for words—
just a growl of gravel to scatter the birds.

WOUNDED KNEE CREEK: HAKIKTAWIN'S STORY

From under my shawl I was watching.
The medicine man did not throw dust
into an officer's face. There was no dust
on that prairie frozen hard as the creek,
where the old people said Crazy Horse
lay buried in a secret place.
One by one our fathers' rifles were stacked
in the circle the wagon-guns surrounded,
but Yellow Bird danced the last ghost dance
steps, telling us the bluecoats' bullets
would not come toward us. Black Coyote,
the deaf one, still clutched a gun inside
his blanket, and when a soldier tried
to take it, began yelling out
what it had cost him, till the soldier
grabbed it, spun him around, and we heard
one rifle crack—then the thunder
without end: all of us running through
powder-smoke and stunted pine and blur
of terror, down toward the ravine I thought
we might still lift across like
a flock of birds rising toward the ghosts
who waited. Instead, everyone was falling.
I saw my grandfather sprawl, then my brother
and grandmother too in the crooked gulch,
and then my hip tore clear through,
and my right wrist burst as I dropped.

Afterward, the cold helped. I lay a long
time listening, till finally only the wind
could be heard, scouring coarse snow
into blizzard. Later a bluecoat picked me up,
carried me to a small girl who rolled
to me, curled into my shawl.
I closed my eyes, listening to the little
sounds she made: not words, not weeping,
but the same faint, chirping phrase—
rising and falling, as if answering itself
from a long distance.

SEVENTIES, USD

Cut loose from our dust-stung towns and farms,
we were daze-walking dreams of becoming
somebody else by finding out what the world
might actually be—*Slaughterhouse Five, Soul
on Ice, Zen and the Art of Motorcycle Maintenance,*
professor-speak and smoke, incense, Crosby, Stills
and Nash humming us back from class or cafeteria
along the tennis courts where maple trees lit up colors
we hadn't known the faded few hundred wheatfields west
we still caught rides home to on weekends with anyone
driving, preferably the long way around, and not
the straight shot across the Reservation's junker-road—
bag-of-bone car-chasing dogs and tumbleweeds, blank
windows, or broken, once two sunken-shouldered kids
dragging a rifle across the side of the blown-over
trailer house never righted those four years; sometimes
one of the old ones scuffing along the gravel toward us
not seeing us—creviced face impassive as the prairie
on either side—or Tribal Police bearing down
from behind suddenly, no telling what they might
decide to pull you over for, who they thought you
could possibly be in your late-model car.

But it was a rattletrap one time—Bruce Chasing Hawk
needed riders to chip in for gas, and Pam and Neal and I
threw our bags in, not about to suggest he skirt the Rez,
though maybe he secretly hoped one of us might ask,
so he wouldn't have to cross that stretch with a carful

of whites who might never have changed a flat,
himself the only Indian—only Indian in our dorm,
hometown boy, our high school's basketball star
nobody, not even the coach, had much spoken to.
But I remembered Bruce—he might not have remembered
me—from long before, the night in grade school when his
little brother fell—got kicked, my dad said later—through
a missing riser in their basement-apartment stairs.
I'd been riding with Dad when the rescue squad radioed;
by the time we got there, Bruce had pried loose two steps,
jumped down with a towel and ropes for lifting the boy,
but their mother hovered above as if she'd just
arrived there in the chairless living room
close with smoke and her white boyfriend's sudden
absence, banter of the Jackie Gleason show
still on with no picture. I looked away
when the men brought the limp boy up, but we heard
he came-to in the admitting room later, that then
the three of them were gone—a different direction
from the boyfriend, Dad said. At sixteen
Bruce appeared in town again, alone, having learned
up at Cheyenne how to shoot even bent-up hoops,
and where a kid needed to play to get a scholarship.

Pay Bruce the gas-money, my folks told me, but find
another ride back to school. Now and then on campus
after that I'd wave; he'd raise a hand. Sophomore year
my RA and her priest took me to a Rosebud

powwow, and Bruce walked over from the bleachers,
stood next to me—one of six whites there—
gave me a piece of fry-bread. Too much clamor
for talk; we watched battered cowboy boots
dancing drumbeats in the dingy gym, old women's
shawls shaking fringe to the songs, till a young man
with braids and a caved-in cheek loomed beside
Bruce, shoved a jacket at him, and angled
back through the crowd. Bruce followed him
to the door in the hall behind, and both glanced around
again; Bruce looked at me. In their two faces
I saw the same heavy eyes and narrow chin,
and realized they were brothers. Then the door swung
open, the two of them stepped through—I felt
a rush of nausea as the glare of late prairie sun
glinted along a gun barrel behind them. The door
slammed shut in time with the drum, the dancing,
the chant's pound like the beat of my fear at turning
back—no idea if anyone had seen, or should—much
less idea how many of the chanters would vanish
on Pine Ridge that decade, uninvestigated, found face
down in gullies or pastures, one with her hands cut off.

Father Mark's truck bumped back the Rosebud road
through gritty half light, then in darkness to the river
and across Yankton; I closed my eyes, still hearing
the big drum on its side, throbbing below taut voices
that rose to catch at a higher pitch before

cutting back down—saw boots circle and lift again,
worn soles flickering in and out of sight, and then, from
two years back, the startling suddenness of Bruce's
moves on the basketball court: feet and hands at a pulse
no eye could anticipate or follow—they'd think they
had him covered, and he'd show up someplace else.

THE CLIFF SWALLOWS

Missouri Breaks

Is it some turn of wind
that funnels them all down at once, or
is it their own voices netting
to bring them in—the roll and churr
of hundreds searing through river light
and cliff dust, each to its precise
mud nest on the face—
none of our isolate
human groping, wishing need could be sent
so unerringly to solace. But
this silk-skein flashing is like heaven
brought down: not to meet ground
or water—to enter
the earth and disappear.

FLY-FISHING ON TOMMY'S LAKE

to Dan

For long intervals the five of us
are silent in the little boat,
drifting, taking turns with the rod,
trying to get the trick,

let the line flick out to its end
above the water, to touch
the fly down first, as if
it's just stopped buzzing there.

I pass the rod to Nan as Tommy lifts
an oar to nudge us clear of a shallow spot—
he must think of Rachel's staying back
at the lake-house after all—*to knit booties,*

she joked. How cautious with her body, so
this second child won't be lost to them.
Nan joggles the line from a snag and we rock a bit;
some minnows shimmer out from under the boat;

a loon's evening-coming-on laugh echoes,
and we all look up. "—To *themselves* they're not spooky,"
murmurs Paul. He checks the fly before Nan casts again.
The two of them, wedged in the prow,

sit closer than they ever do.
How affair-strained years haven't

torn them utterly, no one can know.
Is it possible to get accustomed

to the lens of grief, stop noticing
the way it darkens everything?
I glance at you, then your reflection:
the long brow so like your father's glints

below the blunt end of the boat,
below your effort at looking out
to the world as it is, untouched by sorrow.
Are you watching the pines' jagged shadows?

—A wreath. A shawl drawing round us
in the dimming light. But again last night
you woke with your own crying-out,
drenched, banished from that kitchen

where your father wavered in the doorframe
with his gun—alive, giving you
this chance to stop him.
Over and over the violence of waking

to remember that it's done.
Three months he's gone. You're just trying
to have a weekend with old friends.
Out in the trees' crosshatching

cicadas begin. Nearly dark.
Nobody wants to row back in.

Nan hums a song we all years ago
knew the words to, and Tommy

takes the rod again:
hardly a change in the lake's surface
as the line *whings* and *whings* across.
That's the idea—that's what you want—

not a fish caught, but calm water.
And this single motion over and over,
approximating a delicate ease
we want to believe is nature's.

SECRETISSIME, PRAESENTISSIME

for Mia

Most hidden, most present, like Saint
Augustine's notion of the divine,
soul of my soul, flickering right in front
of my turning to the counter peeling
vegetables while behind shimmers this
hummingbird-jewel, most known ungraspable wing
singing "Jingle Bells" to your popsicle-
stick dolls as you serve up their pudding
of pinecone and carrot snips, miraculous
balancer on the arms of two chairs,
miraculous to have formed inside and grown past
my worry, wash hands don't take dares,
do leave, tiny propeller of sugar and ruby
and air, leave the weight of me behind, but stay.

THE GIRL WITHOUT HANDS

Grimm

Sure enough, I hear the old
I told you so:
Now that you have a child—

now how do you like these stories
of the parents who unwittingly
bring their children to misery,

and need to be forgotten?
What saved the girl, if saved
she was, was her weeping. And not

just once; twice the tears falling
onto her hands, then the stumps
of her hands, washed them too clean

for the devil to go near—
he had to threaten her piousness
through others. The miller,

the girl's father, had no thought
of harming anyone, least of all
his daughter. What

can he have wished for but to feed
his family? When there is no grain,
a miller has nothing. Who in need

doesn't hope for a lucky turn? Who
hasn't once overlooked the glint
in a generous eye, or failed to

wonder *what could this fellow want,*
what's standing behind my mill besides
the old apple tree? The miller bargained it.

His daughter was what stood there
in the mill yard, sweeping.
Now when a weeping child speaks with more

authority than the parent, who has
made a grave mistake,
how can the man ashamed refuse?

Do as the devil says: lift your axe, Father—
God will protect me. Afterward he begged her
not to walk off through the heather,

but in the end it's the parents who give in.
So how was it, when the king
found her pulling down

the pear with her mouth—how was it
she could say to him, she who had set out
away from home so resolute,

"All save God have deserted me"?
In time she too had a child she
bundled away, the boy

named Sorrowful, refugee
hidden in the house with the sign above
"Here everyone is free."

SECRETS

to Mia

Even before a word is on my tongue,
lo, Lord, thou knowest it altogether.
                    Psalm 139

1.

The swans snap up the chunks of bread, then veer
away again, and you call the swans' forgotten
thank-yous across their wake. Slowly stirred
water clears, the way darkness does in your room
when I wait for my eyes to adjust,
for you to take shape under my hand.
The nightmare dissolves;
I will never know what it was.

2.

"I'm making a secret!" you announce,
warming and molding a piece of beeswax
with awkward little fingers, having just learned
that thrilling word I pray will never do you harm.
"Don't look," you say, "don't see it."
Then in a minute, proudly, you display
the gold-red flamelike shape.

3.

I'd forgotten the boy in London yelling at
the black swan, the only black swan I've ever seen.
He wanted it to stop nipping, bullying the other swans
away from his crumbs. *Make it go away,*

138

he pleaded with his father, but finally
it was the boy who went away. I stayed, watching
the black swan left alone, thinking of the black
Rosetta Stone I had been to see one last time that morning,
and shivered in December mist, wanting to be taken
away too from that place of half light, taken back
to your father who wasn't your father yet,
whose steady voice over the phone
cleared the shadows I couldn't talk about.

4.
In "Sweet Porridge" it's a lovely secret
the girl's given: magic words to make the pot
cook up food she and her mother might die without.
And when the mother tries the spell by herself,
her not knowing the right order is also delightful—
porridge out the window, porridge down the walk
and through the streets of the town, so that anyone
who came in from the fields had to eat his way home.

5.
I'd changed the lock on my apartment,
and a whole new doorknob had to be put on.
The handyman laid all the brass pieces out
on a sheet of newspaper—delicate shapes that
would fit together precisely to let only me
into that place. While he worked, he told me
about his wife and daughter, how he didn't know

what to do to keep them apart from each other.
The door stood open, and behind him
the evergreen outside was thrashing. I pictured
the girl's freckles and spaghetti straps, thick red hair
rippling in the truck window the day before,
when Jay had come to make his estimate.
Her mom's visitation rights had been taken away
for using her as a decoy in petty robberies.
Jay and I tried to figure out what to do
with a teenage girl who refuses to talk to you. When
the lock was together then, he handed me the key.

6.

Ten years I hid, at the back of my closet shelf,
a little book I'd received in a moment of fear.
I had gone with a friend in the grade ahead of me
along to her church, having no idea what the word
evangelist meant. The howling minister pointed me out
as one who needed saving, and my friend nudged me up
toward the altar to be touched with the water and
take the book. When I found it again I was eighteen:
just a little volume of the *Psalms*, but it still
unnerved me—*Thou knowest me right well;*
my frame was not hidden from thee,
when I was being made in secret,
intricately wrought in the depths of the earth.
Thy eyes beheld my unformed substance;
in thy book were written, every one of them,
the days that were formed for me,
when yet there was none of them.

7.

Not long before she made herself die,

before she lost herself to grief entirely,

your grandmother watched with your dad and me

the ghostly sonogram knot of you glowing

in my belly. "What a beautiful secret," she gasped,

released for a moment into astonishment.

She left no note in the mountain-house, but we kept

the cut-out shadow-birds she had hung in the windows

to keep live birds from slamming themselves into

their own reflections. She'd dreamed, one night

after her husband's death, of his motioning to her

from the other side of a glass door.

8.

Some night that's coming

I'll hear your voice in my sleep

and stumble to your room to know what it is

you're calling out, but you'll be in a room

someplace else, in a body longer than mine

probably, though maybe you'll still

sleep under the quilt you love now—

patched-together scraps of my childhood curtains

and outgrown pedal-pushers, Mom's aprons, doll

dresses you fit your own dolls into

long after mine disappeared. And if someone else

is there in the room with you, I ask only

that he love you, and the words on your tongue,

and the words still unspoken.

from   BAD RIVER ROAD (2009)

WINDOW

The window of her last room,
in the subacute ward, building
next door to death, was lovely in
the evenings, after visitors had
come and gone, after Dad
had taken Brad back to the farm
and made his last stop in, and
all the machines and tile faded
as snow outside grew violet, then
white against the dark, a steady
glow beneath us. I could leave
the curtains apart while she slept
more heavily with the bigger night
dose of morphine, and I gave up
reading my Chekhov story.

After the first days she hardly
opened her eyes, and the sky
had clouded over, so I left it there
all the time, that square of world
we seemed to have known before,
though we'd never been there.
Now I picture snow stark, definite
against the trees, then realize, no:
it was just September; even in
South Dakota an early snow
wouldn't stay on the ground

that long. Maybe there wasn't
any snow, only the pale light,
and her window altering
the way light passed through it.

BLIZZARD

No seeing to the streets, where our Dad's out
in a national guard truck, moving families with no heat

to the cots and blankets and tinned food at the armory.
Our house warm enough, weirdly muffled inside

the wind, but out front the snow-fort we kids packed
and iced with matted mittens just days ago is vanished

into white frenzy. Mom watching too, maybe wondering
when or how he'll be back—guard, rescue squad,

fire crew, he's always getting called to a body in the river,
a lightning-blazed line of haystacks. Any minute

the fire-radio might pitch its squeal from the kitchen, then
the raspy station-voice repeat again and again the address

to rush to—now and then if I've wandered from bed
Dad takes me in pajamas to hook up the blue flasher

while he veers through stop-lights or barrels beyond town
to where I can look out at a life gone suddenly dark—

black-suited divers under the condemned bridge
searching for Linda Frye; Dad shaking upside-down

the Reese boy with the Lincoln-log piece stuck
in his throat. Other nights the radio spells out

its scratchy directions, but only the rest of us wake up—
those nights he's gone already, his own emergency.

STRABISMUS

E.R.

When the mother first began to notice,
she thought her own eyes must be

playing tricks. *Honey, look at me,*
she'd say, and her daughter would turn

her head, eyes focusing together once
again. But when the child was tired, or

watching TV, one eye strayed, as if
gazing at some secret other scene.

Eventually an appointment was made,
but nothing came up about how she

always squinted in the sun, that even
inside she liked closed closets or

the space behind the furnace—curled up
away from the light under a bed—

sometimes she was impossible to find.
Why would an eye-doctor ask if

a collarbone felt crooked, or a wrist—
if a head might have been slammed, say,

into crib-bars, or swung against a wall,
when a mother wasn't even there to see?

BURNING COAL AT YOUR EAR

to my daughter

You're right, fling it back to
me, lovely brilliant, searing,

clearer-headed than I ever
could've been, running-from-

the-room leggy half-goddess,
core of my heart, furious: yes,

and who can live with it—every
jagged singe, raw *you, why,*

how—you know the precise
level of timbre, flame, know

better, my god, than
I do now—and the truth—

you cover your ears, right to
invoke silence, voice beyond

voice—*is* there a deity with
some correcting trick to hurl it

all the way back through the
corridors of years, each turn

and shadow screaming that
the first terror-scorch,

initial flare, was not, is not,
was never *you*, not *you*

but *I* of course, self-melting
crucible, where you have

had to try and learn
you-from-I—my precious,

hot forehead, forgive me
one day.

THE POND

A little cool, you think,
    then the iron-scent takes you in,
        you leave your feet and let it—

early summer chill easing its ripple
    across your chest as if this water
        never held a body other than yours

—silk, silty touch, thick with
    minerals that knew you before
        your body was body at all—was

nothing, pure impulse, wanting to be
    taken, known, sweet-weight lifted
        alone out to the dark middle,

place you always knew, as it knew
    you would find yourself here, wet,
        untethered, eyes closed, forgetting.

FLOATER

to Dan

Maddening shadow across your line of vision—
what might be there, then isn't, making it

hard to be on the lookout, concentrate, even
hear—well, enough of the story I've

given you, at least— you've had your fill, never
asked for this, though you were the one

to put a hand out, catch hold, not about to let me
vanish the way of the two you lost already

to grief's lure. I'm here; close your eyes,
listen to our daughter practicing, going over and over

the Bach, getting the mordents right, to make the lovely
Invention definite. *What does mordent mean,*

her piano teacher asked— I was waiting in the kitchen
and overheard—*I don't know, something about dying?*

No; morire means to die, mordere means to take
a bite out of something—good mistake, she said.

Not to die, to take a bite—what you asked
of me—and then pleasure

in the taking. Close your eyes now,
listen. No one is leaving.

WAITING IT OUT

Sometimes when the morphine kicks in
Mom thinks Brad is Bud, her twin brother

gone a year now, buried up at Eagle Butte—
boots and cowboy hat in the coffin, then once it

was lowered, the cigarette packs and tins of chew
his sons-in-law tossed in after, swearing

they'd quit for him. At the service
the minister asked for stories, and most

of what came to mind included Mom—
the two of them tiny, not yet lifted down

from the saddle, vanishing in a cloudburst
on their dad's spooked horse;

soaking together in tomato juice
after skunk-hunts; slipping their older

sister's love-letters from her drawer
to memorize and quote at dinner;

chickens pinned down in the barnyard on
their backs, wings open, to hypnotize;

the rolled-up dungarees, skinny elbows and knees
matched to win a county jitterbug contest.

153

Mom knows twin stories—Monty Clift
to Plato to the Yankton—two souls separated

then finally joined again. Bud's marriage
and hers both doomed, both come to an end,

now she's waking to see Brad here
beside her bed—*Bud's' getting*

excited, she says. He pats her leg through
the blanket.—*Are those streamers?* she asks.

—*That's the wallpaper, Mom,* he explains,
bright colors to cheer you up.—*Bud's*

gonna have a party, she whispers, eyes half
closed. *Tell them I'm happy enough.*

KIDS RUNNING DOWNHILL

Howls along a pasture road; jagged

shadows rippling cheat-grass, each leaning back a little

against gravity, except the one in front who's hit

the place where fence rails sag

and start curving up toward the wide

field where he decides

he's got to fall. He knows

in the heat the rest will drop once he does—noise

of mockery, breath heaving,

then finally quiet—turkey buzzards above

wheeling on thermals,

tilting, scanning for carrion—

nothing more, nobody thinking this a thing

to remember—who decides about remembering?

BICYCLING TO SCHOOL

Voices fade; the wordless air's cool, no dew.
Spruce needles riffle, silent above the park,
glistening in this tipped light like
the fur of big animals still asleep. A few
leaves left on the picnic tables' shade-oaks;
besides their rattle and the ticking spokes,
just a scold from one bird and the moan
of wind over prairie—or maybe that's an airplane
drifted off-course. The anemometer's balls turn,
aimless, on top of the courthouse; rain gauge bone-
empty again. Hawthorns in front of school grope away
from the wind, their bearings lost, spikes blurred by
shadows that keep shifting, softening every surface,
so the boundaries of things are impossible to trace.

SKINNY DIPPING AFTER WORK AT THE DRIVE-IN

No moon; the pick-up's headlights stare
across the river from the bluff above, where
fields of sunflower heads turn away,
waiting for dawn. *It's cold*, yells Amy,
and Brian calls *where are you*
but she squeals *no, get away*, so
he and Tommy laugh, dive under for
her legs again. In March I skated over
this same place, past Farm Island, leaving
my track lines in the snow hard to imagine
now, and even then the water must
have moved like this beneath me, erasing
bodies' outlines, as if everything touched
everything all the time.

HE TELLS YOU ABOUT THE DRESS YOU WORE

Every few years he calls from
someplace new, a better job

with free long-distance, offering
a memory, a sort of kindness you

can't repay, voice from the dark
bringing back tight yellow satin,

lights switched out in the stilled
gymnasium, somewhere under

bleachers matching yellow shoes
you don't know how to grope for,

turned as you are, listening to
another dark, voice like water but

thicker, leading you barefoot out
of the locked building into the fire.

SHOT

Flare of voices and lights
caught, blurred, bodies

spliced, then moving as
though smoke were music,

music twisting in
and out of hair and fingers

next to you, throat-
scorch, burn of each word

as it's spoken, mistake
after mistake charred past

memory, yours, your
father's, anyone's you ever

tried to understand and
the ones they knew

before you or met to
forget you with, curses

gone to ash, blacked out,
but you come back again

and again, waiting for
some turn of current, new

element to sting, dissolve,
take you for good.

CRUSH

for Brad

We were dead bored. Some hot brown room
a hundred miles from home, Eagle Butte
or Dupree, I don't remember who was shut
behind the doctor's doors all that time, or for
what reason; no comics, no window, no talk,
no going out in the thunderstorm, the receptionist
stern, no dime from Grandma for the pop machine—
for the heck of it you spent the tedium pulling
anyhow on an Orange Crush that wouldn't budge
from its locked-in position, but you always had
some stubborn gift for hope, a way through any
ill-starred episode, though you kept to yourself
about it, so nobody stopped you, and you didn't stop,
twisting, shifting, closing the cool narrow glass door
a while to whisper at it, then trying again, quick
yanks, long breath-held draws, sudden jerks again, again,
then tugging behind your back. Grandma resolutely
reading her magazine. A rest, then more coaxing to
loosen it, one more good straight pull with skinny arms
and damn if you didn't wrench the thing out unbroken
to gasps all round the waiting room—and who
could stop you then from drinking it? But you offered
me—astonished good-example girl, the one so sure
there could be no surprises, knew how to sit like stone
as if expecting whatever strangeness came along—

you gave me anyway a swig, and your little grin, and
then was it Grandma or some stranger finally
breaking down with a dime after all,
a bottle for me too, since I'd been so still, lifted
not a finger, wasted nothing on luck or any effort
to slip from the nowhere that had us fixed?
Cream Soda for me, since orange pop recalled
the long cartoon spot I'd never be able
to blink or blot out of Mom's wall-to-wall carpet,
even though the blame had wound up with you,
wiggly unpredictable one sent to us to absorb all
guilt, all screaming and shoving around, however
the rake got left beneath the car, or lighter fluid
dripped to the lit grill, or I went for aspirin
and downed instead Mom's sleeping pills—all night
out on the living-room floor, Dad stumbling in over
my feet, four a.m., back from his poker game,
and still I slept, the long spill myself that time—
wasn't there a way to blame you for that too, as if
I were a pile of blocks or a truck you'd left
in the doorway, as if you should have known
to rig a chain across the medicine cabinet, or
conjure some rescue from the TV you stayed
locked to—the Man with the Million Dollar Check
maybe, or Paladin, The Lone Ranger, the All-
Nighter, Prince Good-Heart Charming, Mr. Gone—
none of us understanding you were him all along,
flipping every channel to undo the spell, whip
the rabbit from the sink or the garbage pail, trying

any trick or potion you happened on to, hands
shaking, fingers snapping, to break us out
of whatever it was pressing in from all around—
why should you have had to scream—*wake up,
something's wrong, my eye is black, wake up,
my ear is shot, look, wake up in there, the car's
wrecked, my legs burnt, corn's dried up, tractor
busted, speech slurred, wife gone, hands
cuffed, heart stopped—stone, wake up—
who the hell is in there anyway, asleep?*

SMOKE-BREAK BEHIND THE TREATMENT CENTER

End of the third week: family weekend.
The smokers, most of the patients, are more

jittery than usual, more anxious just now
than other days to step out this door behind

the cafeteria, where they can look across
to the stubble-field, world of chopped-off stalks

that has ripped them up, that they've needed
too much from. In fifteen minutes they'll see

the ones who've come to find out if
they are changing. Maybe half have family

visiting; fewer than that will leave in another
week without needing to come back, to stand

here in a different season and stare at the silo
you set yourself by, imagine walking through

your own cloud of smoke to clean blank sky.

YOU DRIVE OUT TO ASK WHAT THEY WANT
BECAUSE YOU KNOW

it's narcs parked out past the wind-break.
They say they were watching the sunset:

right. Tuning it in with their long-range
antenna, no doubt. The one's Kadlecek—

you knew it, new neighbor down the road—
federal job, he'd said, hunted pheasant in your

corn last fall; borrowed your county atlas
and never returned it. He's the one, probably,

went through the house last week, when you took
a night in the slammer after drifting your truck,

as the trooper explained, over the lane-line.
Hunting-guns confiscated the same night with

spoons and needles and the scale—but they're
waiting for more, thinking you might be bait

for something bigger. So you're waiting too—
tomorrow, or a year, or never—while the phone

is dead that was hopping not long ago,
when you were off your head with forgetting

divorce, kids gone, crops withered
and cattle worthless, what else in the pity-pot?

—your old man still calling you good-
for-nothing kid at forty. When the hay-rake

nailed your foot to the field, somebody
finally came by. Irrigation-pump blasted once

and set you on fire, lit you up good, jumping
fifty feet to the river, trying to remember

if it was deep enough there. Drying
out for real, though—cleaning up—was worse;

easier to just keep vacating your mind.
The shit these guys were after was gone

last week when they broke in for it, but still
could hit the fan if they find someone who'll

drop your name to save his own.
Antenna-car's drifted off now; dust hangs

over the road. No sound, not even from
the moon-high coyote scared of no man.

LAST TRANSFER BACK TO SIOUX FALLS

for my mother

It was a simple thing: the nurse showed me
twice in one minute how to switch the tanks,
the tube, set the reading and flip the pin,
but I was nervous—a three-and-a-half hour
drive, two tanks of two hours' oxygen: I had
to get this small thing right for you; the town's
ambulance was gone a hundred miles
for someone else. Dr. Meyer said we'd be fine,
but he didn't realize you needed to see Brad—
we didn't know when he'd be taken
to prison—the Feds wouldn't let him
leave the farm now to go anywhere,
not the hospital in Pierre, much less
Sioux Falls, even to visit you—we'd have to stop
out east with him, then take the Crow Creek
road down through the Reservation
—I couldn't remember: a gas station partway
at Fort Thompson or Chamberlain. That was
my plan, and the nurse got us downstairs,
wheeled you toward the front, then who
would believe it, Sue at the discharge desk said
the radio had issued a warning, tornadoes
spotted east-southeast—and through the plate-
glass we could see sky black on one side,
vile, blustering. I ran out to the car, pulled it
around, then got the door as the hospital's
SLOW sign whacked over behind the nurse,

her arms lifting you from wheelchair to
front seat. She tucked the blanket round and said
good luck, closed the door, stepped back.

—*Go home.*
Mom, no, we've got to hurry now.
—*I have to go home.*
There's only time to stop with Brad:
look at the sky.
—*There's something at the house I need.*
They'll have everything at the hospital
in Sioux Falls.
—*Please.*
What is it? I'll run in; it's too much
with the tank, you're hardly walking. Is it
something we could get from Brad at the farm?
—*At home. You couldn't hold your eyes open.*
But what?
—*I don't know. I have to see.*
We'll run out of time Mom—
—*I can't go to Sioux Falls if you won't first*
take me home.

Inside we teetered and halted, around your
room, then the bathroom; found your old
flowered make-up kit, and I picked it up, but
you kept looking. Room to room we shuffled,
stood briefly: kitchen, family room, hall, until
it seemed enough. I got you and the oxygen
into the car again, the blanket for your shivering;

you looked up at the house without you in it,
then closed your eyes until the farm—Brad
bolting out through the squall to hug you,
making you laugh somehow, saying everything
would come around all right, then standing at
the gate, drenched, watching as we drove back
down the rutted road and turned toward
the thunderhead churning. You breathed shallow
inside sheets of rain; slept straight into the storm.

GRANDMA HAZEL'S LACE

Root-craze, carrot-frond, tumbleweed racked
by wind, bloodshot eyes awake after days of
dust storm, or after nights of hard-stilled gin

—every kind of nothing looped up by her
hands and tatted into half-hitch lark's-heads,
double-stitch, gap, picot—thread wrapped

on one hand while the shuttle tipped back
and forth, back and forth in the other,
between them a ring of knots forming, a chain,

a wreath, little swath of collar-fancy grown,
or doily, or edging fit for the bedding of the next
bride and groom, who would in turn make

something out of nothing in this no man's land:
house of sod, doll of washcloth, scrap-quilt,
poultice of weeds, butter churned from the one

cow's givings and molded into rose-pats; goose-
down pillows, pheasant-feather hats, and this
magic of laces that we can pick up in our hands,

that we watched take shape above her lap, such
handkerchief frills to catch the eye or heart of a
prince, should ever one pass through these parts.

THE DOOR

She never said *I'm going to die.* I was with her nearly
every minute that week, reading, sleeping on the cot beside

the high-tech bed that kept shifting her slight weight
while the window shadowed over, then grew brighter,

and she drifted or got changed or was given another
shot. None of us said it, though finally when

she was barely talking anymore, I asked something like *Mom,
are you ready?—I just want Brad to be ok* was what

she replied. I told her he would be, as if her wish
or mine could preside at his sentencing hearing.

After that she was almost entirely silent, but when Dad
came the last afternoon, edgy without a cigarette,

checking over the monitors, Mom said she wanted to see him
for a while alone, and he was startled. *Pull the door*

closed, I heard her tell him, and he did. Out in the hall,
staring at the pattern of alternating tiles, I thought of Saturday

mornings when Brad and I were little, and Dad and Mom's
room would be not just shut for a time, but locked. Secretly

I tried the knob once. In that house nobody was allowed
to lock a door but Dad. Grandma would shoo us to the TV

with cinnamon toast to watch cartoons, one fool panic after
the next—bolted dungeons, lies and threats, a saw-blade

inching toward the tied-up body. Then real people like us,
finally: Roy Rogers saving them with his amazing calm.

EVERY NIGHT

Federal holding cell, Hughes County jail

Fights. Never quiet—like years back
with the folks, but ratcheted-up, bloodied,
multiplied, till the guard writes the last two
shovers up, says he'll do the same for all of us
if we can't keep the crybabies smothered
I WANT SOME PEACE,
SLEEP, NO MORE GETTING
OUT OF THE CHAIR, IT'S BAD ENOUGH
WATCHING YOU FOOLS ON
THE MONITOR, NEXT TIME I'LL SHUT
THE TV OFF IN HERE FOR YOU,
GIVE YOU A REASON TO COMPLAIN

—do that. Myron's dull voice from under
his blanket above me, only sound from
up there in two days except his climbing down
for hotdog-chow or a crap—only guy no one
yells at when he's on the shitcan—
someone every hour stinking this cage
of sixteen waiting to be shipped, strung out,
on top of each other every minute—bunk,
shower, shitter, picnic table, TV remote to
fight over, that's it. I thought machinery'd
ruined my ears already, but 24-7 banging
and shouting has them way more gone.
Myron's working on hearing nothing. Finally
weather over 75, so they were taking us out
thirty minutes a day to watch a 20 X 20 patch

173

of sky framed by concertina, till one guy's pal
tossed a pack of Pall Malls over—*leave those
alone* Myron hissed, but that was it, everybody
shaken down; no more light and air.

Now tonight they throw in a fish, kidnapped
his own kid or something *HOW
CAN THEY TAKE HER* slamming
his arms at the bars till they're bleeding,
then old Buffalo yelling *AIDS! GIT 'IM
OUTA HERE*–hammers his own fists
on the steel for the hack to come, clank in,
lock the TV off and turn his back on
two bulldogs in the corner working
the fresh guy over—*SHE'S MY KID,
FOR GOD'S SAKE—FORGET GOD
DIPSHIT, YOU'RE IN NOW, YOU'RE
A GONER* and Buffalo cranking the shower
*STOP THE BLOOD, THROW 'IM IN
THE SLIME, I TELL YA, KEEP
'IM AWAY FROM ME*
till Fuzzy pulls a shank and shuts him up.

Myron groans, rolls over, whacked-out Scott
snores on, *peace, sleep, chair,* the turnkey's
words echo long after the last shudder of bars
—it's all I wanted too, to find the stuff that would
take me out—*peace, sleep, chair,* close as it gets
to lullaby in here, close as any of us ever
got maybe—TV black, our own soundtrack
jagging and vibrating till god knows when.

DAYS END

Slow-play the racket,
bar-banging choir of rage

and threat, white-lit panic—
narrow it, narrow to

the one slit of dusk, window
and beyond, honey-locust

leaves shivering, then
falling still, gust by gust,

distinction taken back as
black lace hooked from

a single spool draws
tighter, knotted fabric

coming not to pieces but
together, closing, gathering

density like water that
rises to make outside,

inside the same: blind
passage anywhere.

WHAT'S LEFT

Six months after our mother's
death, our father's house will burn,
then after six more months, balking,
insurance parts at last with

money to rebuild, and the place
is turned to less than nothing—not
just destroyed; in its spot
a wholly different structure—halls

and cabinets without a trace of cancer
or spearmint gum; no furnace-room
saving up quilting hoops and crickets;
even the extravagant black lace

of the fire: not a wisp of it left,
which is probably best, at least for
Betty, girlfriend moved in when
melted pillows and nightgowns

have vanished and our rooms become
irretrievable before we can. No need
to wonder what happened to letters
pushed at the backs of drawers, boxes

of pictures of shadowy eyes and brows
anticipating ours, Home Extension and
Blue Cross pamphlets, two little blue
slings that only Mom had the proper

memories for, the rabbit-fur collar and
muff from Uncle Norm not there
anymore to slide a hand into. The bride
doll won by Dad in a poker game, its

hair chopped crooked by our cousin Lois—
it's toast, just like your ninth-grade
yearbook with the black-eye photograph,
the untorn tickets from *Romeo and Juliet,*

journal my long-dead boyfriend Keith
entrusted to me, and a mimeographed
Sermon on the Mount I hid after getting
saved and shaking the evangelist's wet

hand. What's left: coins, tools, ashtrays,
some mis-matched earrings, and the can of
arrowheads and tomahawk-heads and
flints Dad and Norm and Marv collected,

wandering to the school at Peoria Flats
that flooded when the dam got built—
those things go back to the Tribe again
finally; and to the College of Mines,

bones of animals we could never
name, and the broken stone with shells
imbedded inside—creatures marooned
by prairie, their ocean gone.

OFFERINGS

Wounded Knee

Years since I'd been back
to the memorial; I'd forgotten

it was up on a rise above
the killing ground. Two kids

appeared in the dust with things
to sell—one coming from the far

end of the chain-link, two kinds
of dream-catchers hanging

from his arm; and the girl, hunched
on the broken steps under

the arch's improbable cross, cradling
a tupperware bowl of beaded

star-necklaces in her lap. Her pink-
and-silver t-shirt read PRINCESS.

I shut my car door, and a grouse
startled off the fence, veered away

over bent switchgrass. The girl—
Allie—said her little sisters made

the jewelry, in the gray house
at the base of the hill; maybe

her price included the pictures I
walked behind her to take: the marker

for 1890, then the more recent
graves, in ground seared and

hardpanned by wind and snow and
desolation; tied bandana-pouches

of tobacco, and ribbons, like fists
and fingers shifting and fluttering;

a few tough bright flowers left;
gray-blue sky rolling above

to the edges of horizon all around,
spitting, cooking up a storm.

I stood and turned back toward
the arch again, where Allie and

her friend, if he was a friend, hadn't
spoken a word to one another.

For the first time in my life
I wished I'd had some cigarettes—

to smoke with them, at least offer,
something to do with strangers you

might sit a while beside till maybe
one of you thought of something

to say. A little thunder crackled,
and we said goodbye; I drove on

toward the shaft of rain above
Manderson.   No reason to think I'd

be any memory to them; a dream-
catcher sold, a brilliant blue

necklace. I passed a knocked-over
vote Democrat sign, and two younger

kids working on a bike upside-down,
and remembered the small bowls,

empty now, brought and offered
at the graves surrounded for miles

by graves never found. Rain would
fill them, lift the reservoirs, clear

the air. I thought of reaching over
to pop the camera-back open; turned

from dirt onto narrow blacktop,
the road out, that was steaming.

LYLE: CONCENTRATION

I don't think anyone was mistreated unless they asked for it.
Sister Mary Francis Poitra, St. Paul's Indian School

Father Joseph showed me this game when we were alone,

all fifty-two cards face-down, and two at a time you tried

to find the pairs, you had to match them. The trick was knowing

what had turned up before, like secrets you'd

glimpsed but didn't remember where—a scar on

someone's shin, but from what ruler; bicycle given

to the boy who wasn't best in school: what did he do? Bitter

lye-soap in your sister's mouth—when did they catch her

speaking Lakota? Stained bloody shorts, bloody paddle;

boy running away, boy hanging by his feet from the bell-

tower; panicked girls under the bed at home, and in the closet,

hidden from the school-boss, then their grandmother lost

the food rations. *Kill the Indian, save the man* was written

above Father Joseph's desk. What man was that? Save what man?

JOHN FAST HORSE: CADILLAC

Past bleached foxtail and bluejoint, sudden flash
of quonset-hut, cutbanks, washouts—half-sideways behind
the wheel, on one knee—other foot stretched to the gas—
miles of dust now between him and the burned
river-front: his foster parents' place. Somewhere northwest, his own
river, the Cheyenne. He'll stick to gravel roads till then;
won't get hauled again to the Agency school—he'll
find Aunt Winnie's trailer if she's still at White Owl.
Wet towels he tried, then a bucket from the trough, till brush-
fire singed up the side of the Cadillac; all he wants is to push
the pedal down now, erase the old man's face trying
trust with him—*Want to ride along in the pick-up to town,*
or stay till we get back? Leave the fireworks in
the box, till the Fourth now, John.

ASH

Wind rakes the bottle-rocket flare
across cliff-grass, ripping the field
off in jagged strips of soot curled
to the sky, as swallows pitch, veer
above the river, then vanish. Quick
as cloud-shadow, this change: beetles
fused, hay and fenceposts blazing back
to what they started as, like the molecules
of the unburned boy who never meant
any damage, who got away but won't
be the same. After a few nights, if
the wind settles, silken ash and mud
mixed with straw and feather-shreds
will line nests hidden under the bluff.

WEST RIVER, DRIVING HOME

Sun low, angling light to pink; heat
beginning to lift finally. Meadowlarks flit
up, away from the car, veering over the ditch
at field's edge where horses stand patient,
paired head to rump, unmoving except for tails
brushing flies from each others' eyes and nostrils.
Sweet corn, then field corn, milo turning but not
ready yet; thick scent of vetch-cover; buckwheat;
a harrow left out where the tractor was last
unhitched. No traffic, but dark quivers in the east—
hint of sheet lightning, memory of Keith face-up
next to me on the ground, the car doors left open
and us flattened under the sky, waiting for wind to drop,
clouds to rain, night to raise us or else turn us to stone.

VIGILANCE

I can call my brother now—no waiting
for the collect prison-phone recording, or
my heart to drop if the connection goes dead

without warning. A day at a time, hour at
a time is how he's free—meth, alcohol, parole
officer's visit—but not of memory, he's quick

to say—what all the mistakes were meant
to end. Last week we walked along the river
at home—he wasn't ready to go out to dinner

yet, or a movie, see people and have to
glance away—so we strolled below the blank
sky, August light easing to dusk, and finally

we could say, without fear of being taped or cut
off, whatever came to mind. Two kids were
kissing in a car pulled up on the causeway, where

the Bad River spills into the Missouri, almost
the spot our parents met; he told me that the day
before his daughter's wedding, before he had to

give his blessing from a bullet-proof booth at the
county jail, he went up to chapel in the examination
room, the one place there with a window, and looked

down through the bars during the volunteer
minister's prayer, watched a couple disappear into
the building next door: Sarah and Charlie,

going in to the courthouse to get their license.
The red hair—what he had first glimpsed
before anyone ever did—when he delivered

Sarah—had made him look twice,
know from the back who it was down there
walking right past, unable to see him

until their fifteen minutes through the glass
next day. We walked as far as the bridge
to Fort Pierre, where he didn't want to cross,

where all the bars stay open an extra hour
for the time-zone change, and he put his arm
across my shoulders to turn us around—strong

rancher's muscle and callus and bone,
its weight making me feel small as
our mom had been, lighter than I am.

LITTLE PARKA

Dream of Mom's red parka gone—
someone stole it right out of the closet
of the burned-down house—what
good could it do anybody else, broken
zipper that always got caught,
she'd jimmy it loose, just part
of putting it on—and she was so tiny,
the arms too short even for me,
too-tiny gloves in the pockets, thumbs
stubby, practically useless to anyone
but her—they deserve it if they shove in
a hand, find the tissue she used and then
left there who knows which cold day,
what she needed it for, or why.

OUTER BANKS

reading Chekhov

Like cool silk billowing, the breeze brushes my arm
and is gone; one after another, spent waves hurry over

the sand as if to offer something, then take it back.
You would laugh if you were here, at the little bi-plane

puttering above the sea to trail its ad, STEAMED
CLAMS AND DANCING AT DAN'S, the letters

threading through the roar that absorbs them and
the puttering, gull-screes, kids' squealing, low voices

of the couple under the nearest umbrella— desperate, it
seems, to solve something after their long walk— still

kissing now and then, running their hands over one
another, but talking on and on, his head shaking as she

covers her face for a time. I look away and read, listen
to the surf's peeling off at an angle from the ocean

in sheets—four huge unravellings repeat, one after another:
lower sounds down the beach, higher, highest right before us,

then deepest beyond, while wind lifts my sleeve and
collar again, trails hair across my face, echoes in my ear

to toy with the birds' tearing cries, children's giggles,
distinct phrase of the man—'we will think of something'—

ribboning over the sand, then drowned in the larger noise
of water borne up from below to wash over us.

NOTES ON THE POEMS

p. 3 "Names Disappearing, Dakota": The place names and Lakota Chiefs' names are from the area that is now central and north-central South Dakota and the Cheyenne River Sioux Reservation, home of the Minneconjou Lakota.

p. 25 "That'll Be the Day": The title recalls the song "That'll Be the Day," written by Buddy Holly and Jerry Allison in 1956.

p. 26 "The River in March, Above Oahe": The Oahe Dam along the Missouri River, just north of Pierre, South Dakota, began generating power for much of the north-central United States in 1962. Named for the Oahe Indian Mission established among the Lakota Sioux in 1874, its construction and resultant flooding took 150,000 acres of prime agricultural land from the Cheyenne River Indian Reservation and 55,993 acres from the Standing Rock Reservation.

p. 36 "Plains: Star Navigation": "Agency School" refers to the Bureau of Indian Affairs school established in Eagle Butte, South Dakota, for the Cheyenne River Sioux Agency.

p. 44 "Dream: The Box Maker and His Brother": Pearl White, an early stage and film actress, lived in the same part of Queens as Joseph and Robert Cornell, and frequently walked her small white pig on a leash along Bell Boulevard, according to Deborah Solomon's *Utopia Parkway*.

p. 51 "Christmas Package: Indigo Pillbox": Emily Dickinson's poem 599 is quoted in lines 4 and 5. A number of Joseph Cornell's works were inspired by Dickinson's poems.

p. 58 "Thank-You Note Worried Over": Lines 8, 11 and 12 quote passages from Anton Chekhov's "The Darling" (Constance Garnett translation).

p. 60 "Asymmetrical Star Quilt for Robert": Robert had "just enough body to keep a soul in"— the artist Solomon Ethe, quoted in *Utopia Parkway*, by Deborah Solomon. For details about the work and lives of Joseph and Robert Cornell, I am indebted to Solomon's *Utopia Parkway*, Diane Waldman's *Joseph Cornell: Master of Dreams*, Charles Simic's *Dime-Store Alchemy* and Jonathan Safran Foer's *A Convergence of Birds*, as well as to the University of Virginia's Fralin Museum, and the Joseph and Robert Cornell Memorial Foundation, whose gifts of Cornell boxes and collages to the University of Virginia have been an invaluable inspiration.

p. 103 "Homesteaders": The Homestead Act of 1862 promised ownership of a 160-acre tract of land in the West to any head of a family who staked a claim, cleared and improved the land, and lived on it for five years.

p. 106 "Regardless of the Final Score": The account of Sitting Bull's assassination is recorded in *Bury My Heart at Wounded Knee*, by Dee Brown.

p. 107 "Keith's Dream": Herbert Zitcalazi was the four-year-old son of Yellow Bird, medicine man at Wounded Knee at the time of the massacre of 1890. He is quoted in *The Ghost-Dance Religion and Wounded Knee*, by James Mooney.

p. 124 "Wounded Knee Creek: Hakiktawin's Story": Hakiktawin was another of the few Lakota witnesses who survived the Wounded Knee Massacre. Her words can be found in Dee Brown's *Bury My Heart at Wounded Knee*.

p. 126 "Seventies, USD": "During the years 1973-1975 more than sixty Indians on the Pine Ridge Reservation—some say as many as three hundred— died violent and unexplained deaths, overwhelmingly from activity instigated by our own Federal government ... as a means of control and domination, some believe acting on behalf of energy interests planning to purloin the reservation's vast untapped mineral wealth, especially uranium." – Ramsey Clark, preface to *Prison Writings*, by Leonard Peltier. For the history of these events I am indebted to

Peter Matthiessen's *In the Spirit of Crazy Horse*. Chasing Hawk is a name that appears also in stories of the visions seen by the Sioux delegation that Red Cloud sent west in the winter of 1889-1890, to learn more about the Ghost Dance Religion. Chasing Hawk was one of their people who had died not long before, and he was seen by the delegates, coming toward them from a very large buffalo-skin tipi, inviting them and all friends to come live with him (*The Ghost Dance Religion and Wounded Knee*, James Mooney).

p. 134 "Secretissime, Praesentissime": Secretissime, Praesentissime: the phrase is from Book One of Saint Augustine's *Confessions*.

p. 148 "Strabismus": Strabismus: a lack of coordination between the eyes, which may result from muscle or nerve disorder, illness, or injury to the eyes or brain, including closed head injuries. In most cases of strabismus in children, the cause is unknown.

p. 181 "Lyle: Concentration": From the 1880s through the 1970s, government and church boarding schools on reservations nationwide carried out a campaign of assimilation based on the credo "Kill the Indian, save the man." Children were removed from their homes by federal agents and taken, often great distances, to live at schools where physical and sexual abuse were commonplace.

p. 188 "Outer Banks": The last two stanzas pay homage to Anton Chekhov's "The Lady with the Little Dog."

BIOGRAPHICAL NOTE

DEBRA NYSTROM was born in Pierre, South Dakota. She is the author of three previous poetry collections: *A Quarter Turn*, *Torn Sky*, and *Bad River Road*. Her work has received the James Dickey Award, the Balch Poetry Award and the James Boatwright Prize for Poetry, as well as fellowships from The Library of Virginia, The Virginia Commission for the Arts, and The Virginia Foundation for the Humanities. She teaches in the Creative Writing Program at The University of Virginia and lives with her husband and daughter in Charlottesville, Virginia.